The CISO's Transformation

Raj Badhwar

The CISO's Transformation

Security Leadership in a High Threat Landscape

 Springer

Raj Badhwar
Ashburn, VA, USA

ISBN 978-3-030-81411-3   ISBN 978-3-030-81412-0   (eBook)
https://doi.org/10.1007/978-3-030-81412-0

This Springer imprint is published by the registered company Springer Nature Switzerland AG
The registered company address is: Gewerbestrasse 11, 6330 Cham, Switzerland

This book is dedicated to the women in my life – to my deceased paternal grandmother, Agyawati Badhwar (Biji) for always being there for me; to my deceased mother, Saroj Badhwar (Mummy), who overcame a lot of personal and family strife while raising me (and my brother); to my deceased Aunt, Reeta Badhwar (Bua), who was instrumental in educating me and giving a professional purpose and direction to my life, my mother-in-law Jackie Meade who has accepted me into the family in spite of my many flaws; and to my multilingual wife, Michelle Badhwar, who helped edit most of the content for this book and has provided a lot of general guidance and support during the process of writing.

I would be remiss if I don't thank my daughter Noelle Badhwar and my son Neil Badhwar for providing me a bouncing off board into the Gen Z mindset and giving me a vision into how teenagers think about technology and security at the current time, and my (younger) brother Kanishka Badhwar (Monu) for all the support and encouragement he has given me all my life.

Foreword

Cybersecurity has become a very prominent and mainstream topic due to audacity, frequency and ease of the attacks & severe disruption, financial and reputational impact caused by them. This is an issue which impacts the society and ecosystem, be it nation state, public & private corporations, or individuals. The Academia, Governments, Regulators, Law & Enforcements, Software/Hardware and Security Services vendors, Ethical hackers, Industry Forums etc. are all trying to do their best to help control, manage and reduce the risks. This has led to a meteorically rise of the role of the Cybersecurity practitioners within the organizations, who find themselves playing a key role in driving this mandate, working across the stakeholders. The Chief Information Security Officer's role has therefore emerged as the main orchestrator expected to lead the way in securing and safeguarding our digital world.

The Cybersecurity industry is very new and faces plethora of challenges such as widening gap between digital innovations and security controls, ever increasing and complex digital threat landscape due to rise and adoption of cloud, AI, IOT, 5G etc., the rise of the threat adversaries and severe shortage of Cybersecurity talent in the industry. The CISO role has evolved to a level which requires a well-rounded skill to ensure success. The CISOs are expected to have executive presence to engage and assure the Board, influencing skills to drive the change across the organization to build a security culture, execution skills to ensure smooth and timely delivery of various organization wide projects, leadership skills to lead large teams of technical architects and security operations to ensure they are all aligned and working for a common goal, business skills to engage and empathize with the business leaders to help secure their business and marketing skills to ensure their vision, mission, values and outcomes are projected to the externals stakeholder effectively & impactfully. This, is by no means, is an easy ask from the next generation Cyber security leaders and therefore it's very important that we collaborate and share our lessons learnt and best practices across our industry and help each other from our experience and mistakes. This book by Raj is one such attempt to help share pearls of wisdom so that young Cybersecurity leaders can benefit and do not have to reinvent the wheel.

I have known Raj for many years now and his vast body of work across different organizations in the field of Cybersecurity has been exceptional. Its applaudable that he has taken time out to pen down his ideas and thoughts in form of this book which could reach to many aspiring CISOs and Cybersecurity leaders. Raj has covered a myriad of Cybersecurity topics in this book and its fascinating to see the diversity of the topics and novelty of the ideas. Raj has covered various dilemmas and challenges faced by the Cybersecurity leadership and provides some great anecdotes, approaches, and pathways to deal with them. Covering topics on different leadership dimensions and decision making for CISOs, hiring to career planning, Cybersecurity biases, common taxonomy, never allow a good crisis to go waste, impactful and engaging conversations, Cybersecurity offence strategies, CISO liability protection, WFH and many more interesting topics, Raj will take you through a very interesting ride which I promise you, will not just be engaging but also rewarding with some great practical thoughts and ideas which you can apply to overcome your challenges.

This is a book for every Cybersecurity professional and also for those who want to empathize with this problem and become a partner is solving this together. Wish you a great read.

CISO & Head of Cyber Security Infosys   Vishal Salvi
Electronic City, Bangalore, Karnataka, India

Preface

The CISOs who are best positioned to protect their organizations from an increasing number of sophisticated threat actors, malware, third-party attacks (like SolarWinds), and insider threats, while also enabling secure product development and implementing a "Shift Left" paradigm, are those with both the extensive technical knowledge and expertise to understand and evaluate the latest security technologies and the vision to assert new forms of CISO leadership and influence throughout their organizations.

My previous (Springer) book, *The CISO's Next Frontier: AI, Post-Quantum Cryptography and Advanced Security Paradigms*, described the various current and future advanced security technologies to empower CISOs to protect their enterprises. This book focuses on how and why CISOs should chart new leadership pathways to improve organizational security and company value, and on how to build and retain excellent cybersecurity talent pools and advocate for cybersecurity hygiene and prudence.

The first section of the book maps out new paths for effective CISO leadership. CISOs of the past tended to come out of backgrounds in physical security or the military, or government policy and regulation. CISOs now add significant value when they also possess an advanced understanding of cutting-edge security technologies to address the risks from the nearly universal operational dependence of enterprises on the cloud, the internet, hybrid networks, and third-party technologies. Today's CISO roles embody aspects of both the past and the future, with the most mature and forward-looking CISOs combining strong business and technical leadership skills. In this threat-saturated environment, the CISO should be a fully empowered senior executive to secure customer data and enterprise systems, provide rapid incident response when needed, provide regulatory compliance, help develop products, enable business continuity, while also helping the firm win in the marketplace. Today, CISOs who create security-related products that address customer security concerns shore up the company brand and add market value. In fact, Wall Street is more likely to reward companies with good cybersecurity track records with higher stock valuations. To ensure that security is always a foremost concern in business decisions, external CISOs should sit on corporate boards, and

CISOs should create an expectation for beginning-to-end CISO involvement in IT processes for adopting (new) enterprise technologies, and in the C-Suite's processes for mergers and acquisitions and expanding business partnerships. While newly hired CISOs are often tempted to show their prowess as a leader and engage in the drama of "shaking things up" by sweeping in a completely new staff built around their own personal connections, they may have more success by inspiring the existing team to work harder and smarter.

The remainder of the book focuses on additional methods of building effective security teams and on exercising prudence in cybersecurity. CISOs can foster cultures of respect for others through careful examination of the biases inherent in the socio-cultural frameworks shaping workplace language and respect for the mission by instilling practices of cyber exceptionalism. To build and retain a strong talent pool, CISOs should leave no stone unturned in seeking out people with unique talents, skills, and cross-functional experience and encourage career planning and development. CISOs should expect their teams to follow a cyber hygiene mantra to reduce the exploitable vulnerabilities of their corporate systems.

The last section includes pandemic considerations on securely working from home, masking in the workplace, and the use of data hashes to track virus variants. The lessons of the breach of physical security at the US Capitol, the hack back trend, and CISO legal liability stemming from network and data breaches, all reveal the importance of good judgment and the necessity of taking proactive stances on preventative measures.

The "CISO Take" at the end of each chapter summarizes the CISO's point of view on the subject discussed, generally identifying an opportunity for improvement or elaborating on the steps needed to be secure in the next technological frontier. Some chapters also have (some) definitions for cryptic terms or jargon that may be unfamiliar to those not in cybersecurity.

Ashburn, VA, USA   Raj Badhwar

Cybersecurity is as much about leadership as it is about technology – Raj Badhwar (2021).

Disclaimer

The views expressed and commentary provided in this book are strictly private and do not represent the opinions or work or the state of and/or implementations within the cyber-security or IT programs of my current or former employer(s). Any advice provided here must not be construed as legal advice. If you choose to follow any advice provided in this book, then you must do so at your own risk.

Acknowledgment

I must acknowledge my dear wife Michelle Badhwar, without her editing prowess and hard work, this book would not have been possible; my daughter Noelle Badhwar for doing one of the illustrations; Dr. Helen McCabe and Karen McCabe of the Five Project for reviewing the chapter on disability; and Deb Dey for reviewing the initial book proposal.

I should thank Steven Dick for introducing me to Springer.

This book was mostly written during the 2021 Pandemic and I would like to take this opportunity to acknowledge the good work done by the cybersecurity professionals worldwide for working tirelessly to enable the secure work-from-home paradigm.

Raj Badhwar

Contents

Part I   Effective CISO Leadership

CISOs – Leading from the Front! 3
1   Introduction. 3
2   Be the Security Evangelist 4
   2.1   Take an Active Hand in Creating the Cybersecurity
       Policy and Standards 4
   2.2   Lead Innovation and Next-Generation Security
       Technology Implementations. 5
   2.3   Secure Cloud Environments 5
   2.4   Make the Case for Security to Both Technical
       and Business Audiences. 5
   2.5   Understand, Assess, and Quantify Cyber Risk 5
   2.6   Lead Tactical vs. Strategic Implementations 6
   2.7   Lead User Training and Communications. 6
   2.8   Be Prepared to React to Cyber-Attacks
       and Other Cyber-Induced Disruptions. 6
   2.9   Make the Case to the Board of Directors
       and Other Executives. 7
   2.10 Recruit and Retain 7
   2.11 Attract Women and Other Minorities to the
       Cyber Security Profession. 7
   2.12 Win the Market Place. 8
3   The CISO Take 8
4   Definitions. 8
References. 9

More CISOs on Corporate Boards 11
1   Preface.. 11
2   Let's Define Cyber Threats and Cyber Risk First.................... 11
3   Making the Case 12
4   The CISO Take 13
5   Definitions... 13
References.. 14

Cyber Program Turnaround by New CISO 15
1   The Human Element 15
2   Use of Security Frameworks.. 16
3   Adoption of a Cloud-Based Security Stack 16
4   Zero Trust 17
5   Seamless Biometric Authentication 17
6   Making Use of Threat Intelligence 17
7   Active Board-Level Participation 17
8   Effectiveness Testing.. 18
9   The CISO Take 18
10 Definitions... 18
References.. 19

CISOs – The Next Step! 21
1   Introduction.. 21
2   Current State for Most Hands-on CISOs 21
3   The Near-Future State... 22
4   The Not-So-Distant Future State 23
    4.1   Cybersecurity Product Development.......................... 23
    4.2   Cybersecurity Services Development 24
    4.3   Cyber Wellness 24
    4.4   Cyber Insurance Certification and Attestation.............. 24
    4.5   How Can This Be Delivered? 25
5   The CISO Take 25
6   Definitions... 26
References.. 27

CISO Maturity Model 29
1   Introduction.. 29
2   The Maturity Model 29
    2.1   The Technical Track.. 31
    2.2   The Business Track 32
    2.3   The Hybrid Track.. 34
3   The CISO Take 35
4   Definitions... 36
References.. 36

CISO Commentary on Some Emerging and Disruptive Technologies. . . .   39
1   Introduction.   39
2   Security Commentary   40
3   The CISO Take   42
4   Definitions.   43
References.   43

See Something, Do Something!   45
1   Genesis   45
2   See Something, Say Something   46
3   See Something, Do Something   47
    3.1   Making the Case   47
4   The CISO Take   51
5   Definitions.   52
References.   53

My Journey as a Writer   55
1   Introduction.   55
2   Early Years   55
3   Technical Writing   56
4   The CISO Take   57
Further Reading   57

Defensive Measures In the Wake of the SolarWinds Fallout.   59
1   Introduction.   59
2   Generic Defensive Measures   59
    2.1   Enable Improved DNS Alerting Using a DNS Sinkhole   60
    2.2   Deploy Malware Kill Switch   60
    2.3   Perform Monitoring and Alerting Enhancements   60
    2.4   Detect Golden SAML Attacks.   61
    2.5   Reconsider the Usage of DOH   61
    2.6   Better Manage Third-Party Risk   61
3   SolarWinds Specific Actions.   62
4   The CISO Take   62
5   Definitions.   62
References.   63

Part II   Cybersecurity Team Building

Cyber Exceptionalism.   67
1   Genesis   67
2   Introduction.   67
3   What is Cyber Exceptionalism?   68
4   Who Can Be Cyber Exceptional?   68
5   How Can One Become Cyber-Exceptional?.   68
6   My Cyber Journey.   69

7   The CISO Take   70
8   Definitions.   71
References.   71

Special Needs, Disability, and Cybersecurity: Often, a Great Fit   73
1   Making the Case.   73
2   The CISO Take   74
3   Definitions.   75
References.   76

Bias-Free Lexicon   77
1   Introduction.   77
2   Shoring Up Professionalism in the Workplace   78
3   What's the Impediment to Linguistic Reform?.   78
    3.1   Response to Impediments   81
4   Corrective Behaviors.   82
5   The Next Step   82
6   The CISO Take   83
7   Definitions.   84
References.   84

The Grass Is Not Always Greener on the Other Side   87
1   Introduction.   87
2   Happiness and Job Satisfaction.   87
3   Don't Burn Your Bridges   88
4   Get a Mentor   88
5   Other Implications   89
6   The CISO Take   89
Further Reading   90

Let Not Any Outage Go to Waste   91
1   Introduction.   91
2   Making the Case   91
3   Change Management   92
4   Operational Ownership.   93
5   The CISO Take   94
6   Definitions.   94
References.   94

If You Can't Hire Them, Then Develop Them   95
1   Introduction.   95
2   Develop the Talent   95
    2.1   Technology Aptitude   96
    2.2   Flexibility.   96
    2.3   Business Domain Awareness   97
    2.4   Mission Focus   97
    2.5   Systems Thinking   97

  2.6   Problem Solving 98
  2.7   Collaboration 98
  2.8   Expand the Net 98
  2.9   Trust.. 99
3 Retention.. 99
  3.1   Entry-Level 99
  3.2   Mid-Level 100
  3.3   Senior and Executive Level 100
4 The CISO Take 100
Definitions.. 101
Further Reading 101

Should You Accept Counteroffers? 103
1 Introduction... 103
2 General Advice and Comments 104
3 Advice to Employees 104
4 Advice to Managers 105
5 The Cybersecurity Skew....................................... 105
6 My Own Experience... 106
7 The CISO Take 106
Further Reading 107

Importance of 1:1 Conversations............................... 109
1 Introduction... 109
2 Guidance.. 109
  2.1   What Is Going Well? 109
  2.2   What Is Not Going So Well?................................ 110
  2.3   Ask for Feedback... 110
  2.4   Give Feedback 110
  2.5   Talk About Opportunities.................................. 111
  2.6   Talk About Career Growth................................. 111
  2.7   Talk About Individual Development 111
  2.8   Brainstorm Ideas 112
  2.9   Skip Level Meetings 112
3 The CISO Take 112
Further Reading 113

The Cyber Hygiene Mantra...................................... 115
1 Introduction... 115
2 Recommendation 116
  2.1   Identify and Patch All High/Medium Risk Vulnerabilities 116
  2.2   Reduce Threat Surface.................................... 116
  2.3   Perform Identity and Access Management 117
  2.4   Enable Asset Protection................................... 118
  2.5   Perform User Training and Awareness 118
  2.6   Setup a Certification and Accreditation (C&A) Program 118

3   The CISO Take 119
4   Definitions... 119
References... 120

Part III   Cybersecurity Prudence

**Cybersecurity Lessons from the Breach of Physical Security at US Capitol
Building** 125
1   Introduction.. 125
2   Best Practices 125
3   The CISO Take 127
4   Definitions... 127
References... 128

**Protect Society, the Commonwealth, and the Infrastructure – Post
COVID-19** 131
1   Introduction.. 131
2   Technical Controls Required to Securely Work from Home, and Back ... 131
3   Number of Masks Required to Securely Go Back to Work 132
4   Virus Tracking (SARS-CoV-2)..................................... 132
5   The CISO Take 134
6   Definitions... 134
Further Reading 134

Self-Service Recovery Options for Bricked Windows Devices 137
1   Introduction.. 137
2   Solutions 137
     2.1   USB Boot Drive.. 138
     2.2   Create a USB Recovery Drive, or Media (DVD or CD) 139
3   BSOD or Bricked? 139
     3.1   USB Boot Drive.. 139
     3.2   Recovery Drive 140
     3.3   Prerequisites... 140
4   Edge Cases 140
5   The CISO Take 141
6   Definitions... 141
References... 142

Certification & Accreditation.................................... 143
1   Introduction.. 143
2   Making the Case 144
3   The Workflow Outline... 145
     3.1   Initiation Phase 145
     3.2   Security Certification Phase.............................. 145
     3.3   Security Accreditation Phase............................. 145
     3.4   Continuous Monitoring Phase 146
4   The CISO Take 147

5   Definitions... 147
References.. 148

Hack Back or Not?... 151
1   Introduction.. 151
2   Genesis.. 151
3   What Is a Hack Back?.. 152
4   Security Issues and Impediments 152
     4.1   Currency... 153
     4.2   Code Vulnerabilities.. 153
     4.3   The Weak Link... 153
     4.4   Sophisticated Attackers 154
     4.5   Lack of Defense Coordination................................. 154
     4.6   Hacking Tools 155
5   Making the Case.. 155
     5.1   Hacker Identities Are Unknown 155
     5.2   It May Be Illegal 155
     5.3   Open Cyber-Warfare 156
     5.4   Friendly Fire 156
     5.5   Asset Retrieval... 157
6   The CISO Take 157
7   Definitions... 157
References.. 158

CISOs Need Liability Protection.. 161
1   Making the Case.. 161
2   Liability Insurance 161
     2.1   Verify Your Coverage... 162
3   Employment Contracts 162
4   State Laws... 163
5   Company Bylaws 163
6   The CISO Take 164
7   Definitions... 164
References.. 165

Enable Secure Work-From-Home... 167
1   Making the Case.. 167
2   The CISO Take 168
References.. 169

Postlude – Paying It Forward 171

Index.. 175

About the Author

Raj Badhwar has 25+ years of experience within the Cybersecurity and IT industry. He is currently the CISO for Voya Financial and has previously held senior Security and IT leadership roles at AIG, BAE Systems Inc., Bank of America, Time Warner Cable, AOL Time Warner, and Sprint. Raj is currently a director and secretary of the board of the National Technology Security Coalition. He also serves on the cybersecurity advisory boards of Pace University, Rutgers University, and Ithaca College; the customer advisory board for Venafi; and the CISO advisory council for Infosys. Raj is a certified information systems security professional (CISSP), a certified ethical hacker (CEH), and a FINRA licensed securities professional (Series 99). He has coauthored 14 security patents and has written and presented in the areas of advanced encryption, post-quantum cryptography, zero trust networks, cloud security patterns, and secure remote work paradigms. He is the author of *The CISO's Next Frontier* another cybersecurity book. He has also been interviewed as a cybersecurity subject matter expert by *WSJ*. Raj is proficient in three languages and conversant in another three languages. Raj graduated from George Washington University (GWU) with an MS in Information Systems Technology and also holds a BS in Electrical and Electronics engineering from Karnatak University. Raj is an alumnus of St Francis College, Lucknow.

Abbreviations

ABA	Applied Behavioral Analysis
ACL	Access Control List
AD	Active Directory
AI	Artificial Intelligence
AP	Access Point
APT	Advanced Persistent Threat
ASD	Autism Spectrum Disorder
ATO	Authorization to Operate
ATOC	Authorization to Operate with Conditions
AV	Antivirus
BCM	Business Continuity Management
BISO	Business Information Security Officer
BoD	Board of Directors
Bot	robot
BRO	Business Resilience Office
BSOD	Blue Screen of Death
C&A	Certification and Accreditation
CA	Certificate Authority
CAB	Change Advisory Board
CBB	Common Branch for Business
CCDA	CISCO Certified Design Associate
CCIE	CISCO Certified Internetwork Expert
CCNP	CISCO Certified Network Professional
CCPA	California Consumer Privacy Act
CEH	Certified Ethical Hacker
CI/CD	Continuous Integration/Continuous Delivery
CIFS	Common Internet File System
CIS	Center of Internet Standards
CISA	Cybersecurity and Infrastructure Security Agency
CISM	Certified Information Security Manager
CISSP	Certified Information Systems Security Professional

CLO	Chief Legal Officer
CMDB	Configuration Management Database
CNC	Command and Control (server)
COVID-19	Coronavirus disease (2019)
CRO	Chief Risk Officer
CSaaS	Cyber Security as a Service
CVE	Common Vulnerabilities and Exposures
D&O	Directors and Officers
DAST	Dynamic Application Security Testing
DC	Domain Controller
DDoS	Distributed Denial of Service
DHS	Department of Homeland Security
DLP	Data Loss Prevention
DMARC	Domain Message Authentication Reporting and Conformance
DNA	Deoxyribonucleic Acid
DNS	Domain Name Service
DNS Sinkhole	Domain Name Service Sinkhole
DNSSec	Domain Name Service Secure
DOB	Date of Birth
DOD	Department of Defense
DOH	DNS over HTTPS
DSS	Defense Security Service
ECAB	Emergency Change Advisory Board
EDR	Endpoint Detection and Response
ELC	Executive Leadership Committee
EMF	Engineering Management Framework
FDaaS	Fraud Detection as a Service
FFIEC	Federal Financial Institutions Examination Council
FINRA	Financial Industry Regulatory Authority
FS-ISAC	Financial Services Information Sharing and Analysis Center
FTC	Federal Trade Commission
FW	Firewall
GDPR	General Data Protection Regulation
Golden SAML	Golden Security Assertion Markup Language
GRC	Governance Risk and Compliance
HCI	Hyper Converged Infrastructure
IaaS	Infrastructure as a Service
IAM	Identity and Access Management
IdP	Identity Provider
IDP	Individual Development Plan
IDS	Intrusion Detection System
IOC	Indicators of Compromise
IOT	Internet of Things
IP	Intellectual Property
IPS	Intrusion Prevention System

ISO	International Organization for Standardization
ISSAP	Information Systems Security Architecture Professional
ITIL	Information Technology Infrastructure Library
IVR	Integrated Voice Response
KBA	Knowledge-based Article
LTSB	Long-Term Servicing Branch
LTSC	Long-Term Servicing Channel
M&A	Mergers and Acquisitions
MaaS	(Security) Monitoring as a Service
MAM	Mobile Application Management
MBA	Master of Business Administration
MDM	Mobile Device Management
MFA	Multi-factor Authentication
MITM	Man-in-the-Middle (Attack)
ML	Machine Learning
NAC	Network Access Control
NAS	Network-Attached Storage
NFL	National Football League
NFS	Network File System
NIST	National Institute of Standards and Technology
NTP	Network Time Protocol
NTPSec	Network Time Protocol Secure
NYDFS	New York Department of Financial Services
OEM	Original Equipment Manufacturer
OOB	Out of Band
OSCP	Offensive Security Certified Professional
OSU	Ohio State University
OTP	One-Time Password
PaaS	Platform as a Service
PAM	Privileged Access Management
PII	Personally Identifiable Information
POA&M	Plan of Action and Milestones
PTH	Pass the Hash
PTSD	Post-Traumatic Stress Disorder
QA	Quality Assurance
RACF	Resource Access Control Facility
RCA	Root Cause Analysis
RFC	Request for Comments
RFI	Request for Information
RFP	Request for Proposal
RIDT	Rapid Influenza Diagnostic Test
RMF	Risk Management Framework
RNA	Ribonucleic Acid
RPA	Robotic Process Automation
RSAC	RSA Conference

SaaS	Software as a Service
SAML	Security Assertion Markup Language
SAN	Storage Area Network
SARS-COV2	Severe Acute Respiratory Syndrome – Coronavirus 2
SCCM	System Center Configuration Manager
SEC	Securities and Exchange Commission
SHA	Secure Hash Algorithm
SIEM	Security Incident and Event Management
SOC	Security Operations Center
SOC 1	System and Organization Controls (Report) 1
SOC 2	System and Organization Controls (Report) 2
SP	Service Provider
SPAN	Switched Port Analyzer
SSN	Social Security Number
SSO	Single Sign-On
STEM	Science, Technology, Engineering, and Math
TAP	Test Access Point
TCP	Transmission Control Protocol
TDE	Transparent Data Encryption
TIaaS	Threat Intelligence as a Service
TLS	Transport Layer Security
UDP	User Datagram Protocol
UEFI	Unified Extensible Firmware Interface
USB	Universal Serial Bus
VPC	Virtual Private Cloud
VPN	Virtual Private Network
WAF	Web Access Firewall
WHO	World Health Organization

Part I
Effective CISO Leadership

CISOs – Leading from the Front!

1 Introduction

The cyber risk and threat landscape has changed rapidly and dramatically over the last decade. CISOs now must address risks, challenges, and demands once inconceivable: the evolution of sophisticated malware, data exfiltration, and breach tools; publicly known and high-profile exploits of internet-facing business applications containing sensitive customer or business data; monetization of the breached or exfiltrated data; the emergence of insider threat; the theft of data and IP by nation states; and ever stricter regulatory guidelines at the local, state, and federal levels enforced through censure, suspension, and massive fines.

It would not be far-fetched to assert that the cyber and reputational risk a given business entity carries today is equal to or greater than more traditional notions of risk from inflation, reinvestment, interest rates, business cycles, capital, finance, currency, liquidity, or legislation.

This changed landscape requires CISOs to manage sophisticated threats proactively. CISOs must be hands-on security technologists with an active involvement in the day-to-day cyber engineering, operations, and incident response activities. In other words, the modern-day CISO must lead from the front –talking the talk and walking the walk. Like generals leading their soldiers on the frontlines of combat, the CISO needs to step out of their back office to train and lead the cybersecurity teams, engaged on the frontlines of a very real modern cyber warfare.

In the past, many CISOs had career backgrounds in the military, industrial security, the military industrial complex, or policy. These CISOs advanced the CISO role by establishing company security policy to comply with government regulations and to protect the company. They also developed good protocols for physical security and risk management. Today's CISOs still need to know policy and physical security, but they also must understand security engineering, which involves the engineering and operations of security tooling, vulnerability management, the

R. Badhwar, *The CISO's Transformation*, https://doi.org/10.1007/978-3-030-81412-0_1

detection and mitigation of APT (advanced persistent threat) and polymorphic malware, threat Intel and associated support platforms and ecosystems, monitoring and response, data security, and identity and access management. They also must stay abreast of the various new ways to detect and prevent the exploitation of vulnerabilities and weaknesses in our internet-facing high-risk applications and associated middleware stacks.

The fact is that CISOs *are* becoming more technical. I am one of those CISO types and carry many security and network certifications. I came up as a developer and systems engineer, implementing various capabilities and technologies, while also writing technical security specifications and standards along the way. I approach my job with this principle: anything that my security engineers, architects, or incident responders can do, I can do it, too. While I now may no longer be as proficient as I once was, to this day I still rely on my technical skills and knowledge as my team and I work together to resolve both broad and specific technical issues and challenges.

Given the expanding role of the CISO, there are multiple areas of command by which successful CISOs lead. To be a successful security leader, you must:

2 Be the Security Evangelist

The CISO must evangelize the importance of application and system security to the broad spectrum of employees and leaders within the given firm. The CISO must lead by example and reach out to IT and Infrastructure teams to partner and collaborate, doing whatever it takes, including educating employees and vendor partners about the Zero Trust security paradigm, about third party risk, risks from sophisticated malware and secure application development by offering company-wide lectures, discussing topics in staff meetings and on the CISO blog, publishing white papers and FAQ's on the company intranet sites, to help build an inherently secure ecosystem and an cyber (threat) aware and educated workforce.

2.1 Take an Active Hand in Creating the Cybersecurity Policy and Standards

CISOs must have an active hand in the drafting/overseeing the drafting of cyber security policy and standards and taking the lead in getting company-wide agreement on the said policy and standards. As instruments of reducing enterprise cyber risk, these cyber security policies and standards must provide means for compliance with local, state, and federal regulations, provide guidance to remediate the current systemic technological vulnerabilities, and how to do secure application and systems development. They are an important means of implementing and enforcing security controls throughout an enterprise.

2.2   *Lead Innovation and Next-Generation Security Technology Implementations*

Hands-on knowledge of security technologies has become more important in cyber-security with increased use of AI and ML-enabled tools and technologies. To a CISO, those concepts can't just be buzzwords. CISOs must understand how to implement and manage those technologies, what threat factors they mitigate, and what threat factors they may introduce into the environment. CISOs must also gauge the value proposition and return of investment from these security technologies.

2.3   *Secure Cloud Environments*

The adoption of cloud computing paradigms (e.g., IaaS, PaaS, and SaaS) has sky-rocketed for almost all business types and domains. Modern CISOs must under-stand how best to monitor and protect data, systems, and applications across the public, private, and hybrid cloud environments. This includes CISOs making the case for and overseeing security pattern architecture, design, and implementation, accomplished in collaboration with the devSecOps and other cloud infrastructure implementation and application development teams.

2.4   *Make the Case for Security to Both Technical and Business Audiences*

I don't see a barrier for a technical CISO here. If you are technical about a given subject, you can probably speak about it non-technically. Technical CISOs can sim-plify the matter at an appropriate level for their audience. However, if you are not technical and you don't understand the subject matter, you cannot answer deeper questions and you'll have to defer them to those with the technical expertise. Technical CISOs, with the appropriate amount of training and guidance, can talk at a high level and get technically deeper when needed, but the reverse is not true.

2.5   *Understand, Assess, and Quantify Cyber Risk*

The CISO must accurately quantify the total amount of cyber risk a company car-ries. Only then they can work on prioritization strategies to determine which part of that risk needs to be remediated, which part needs to be mitigated through the implementation of other security controls (e.g., monitoring, micro segmentation), and which risks need to be accepted by the business. The CISO must also play an active role in devising the cyber insurance or risk transference strategy for a given business entity. The financial quantification of the total cyber risk helps with this decision making.

2.6 Lead Tactical vs. Strategic Implementations

The CISO must take a leading role in distinguishing between which security infrastructure and tooling implementations or enhancements are strategic (towards a target state) and which are merely tactical (to implement an intermediate state) to the reduction of enterprise cyber risk. These determinations are crucial to funding prioritizations as the CISO makes the case to a firm's executive leadership and board of directors to obtain the appropriate levels of funding for cyber security.

2.7 Lead User Training and Communications

The CISO must lead the charge for end user training and communicate best methods for detecting and blocking security threats, especially those coming through high traffic channels with great susceptibility to being compromised. Some topics relevant to company user security training are dealing with the risks of phishing or spoofing on the email channel, recognizing data exfiltration and fraud attempts by malicious insiders or impersonators, categorizing and protecting company sensitive data and IP, and other risks such as (malicious) drive-by-download on the web channel.

2.8 Be Prepared to React to Cyber-Attacks and Other Cyber-Induced Disruptions

The CISO must lead (or be an active participant in) quarterly tabletop exercises to simulate cyber-induced threat scenarios (e.g., ransomware attacks, malware infestation, DDoS attacks, APT etc.) to judge a company's capability to react and respond in an expedient manner.

They must also take an active role in the design, implementation and management of (local and remote) application and system disaster recovery, and business continuity management to account for catastrophic disruptions by malware, network outages, weather events, health events (e.g., the 2020 Pandemic) or natural disaster calamities.

2.9   Make the Case to the Board of Directors and Other Executives

The CISO must be ready and able to present the current state of the security program to the company's board of directors with a proposal for a secure future state where all known risk is either remediated through security controls, mitigated through monitoring controls, or transferred through cyber insurance. The CISO must have a good grasp on the cyber security budget and must be able to present and defend it in front of the board of directors.

2.10   Recruit and Retain

Any security team is only as good as its engineers, operations personnel, architects, cyber incident responders, and risk assessors. The CISO must have the capability to attract, recruit, and retain top cyber talent by providing an innovative and stimulating work environment.

They must also develop good relationships with schools, colleges and universities to attract the cyber security engineers of the future. This can be achieved by starting a security internship program, and shaping the interns to be the employees of the future.

2.11   Attract Women and Other Minorities to the Cyber Security Profession

The CISO must attack the root cause of the chronic shortage of women and minority cyber security professionals by building an interest in cybersecurity for women and other minorities while they are in K-12 and college.

Also, security has always had somewhat of a macho aura around it. That gives the impression that cybersecurity is full of ex-military, ex-defense, or ex-police-type people. It's easy for some people to think their personality may not be a fit in that career. The CISO must break defense and military stereotypes, because cybersecurity is a diverse field also involving policy, operations, architecture, and engineering, along with some people who have defense and military backgrounds. It's a mixed bag. People of all types, ideas, and diversities are welcome here.

[I think the future is bright for the security industry due to awareness and interest in diversity and hiring diverse candidates. Hiring managers are often ready to wait a little longer to get interviews with diverse candidates, rather than just looking at the first five resumes and hiring quickly.]

Diversity is also a mission, and we need to get the message of the mission across. For example, look at our military. We have diverse men and women there. They fight shoulder to shoulder. They have a shared national pride and mission to protect and defend the nation. The CISO must bring a similar mission to the security industry to protect our organization's systems and data. In the financial services industry, we must protect our user data, customer data, employee data, and company reputation. When you impart that sense of mission to the people who work in the cybersecurity profession, you can transcend differences. The CISO can play a key role in evangelizing the mission.

2.12   Win the Market Place

The CISO must help their company win in the marketplace by helping win new business by being able to assert the secure state of their company's data, systems, networks, and applications, and their compliance with any applicable local, state, or federal regulations.

In this age of reputational risk from cyber breaches and hacks, both the (current and prospective) customers and the Wall Street financial analysts have been known to reward the companies with good cyber track records with more business and higher stock evaluations than their unsecure counterparts.

3   The CISO Take

Given the advanced and persistent threat from cyber-attacks and data breaches, the rapid migration to the cloud, the tough regulatory scene globally, hyper convergence of compute and storage, and the "SaaSification" of our corporate systems and application stack dealing with high risk and sensitive data, next generation CISOs must lead from the front to ensure that the confidentiality, integrity and availability of company data and systems is maintained, and help their firms to win the market place, while they continue to help their firms charter through the murky waters of high cyber risk.

4   Definitions

APT – stands for Advanced Persistent Threat. It is used to describe a campaign of attacks by persistent sophisticated threat actors whose intent is to gain long-term residence or presence on the network of the target. The list of malicious activities includes but is not limited to stealing intellectual property or company sensitive data, sabotaging key network segments or systems, installing and operating backdoors to communicate with CnC servers, and conducting complete site takeovers. These attacks are complex, targeted, well-resourced and funded, and are generally conducted by nation states or other criminal organizations [1].

CISO – stands for Chief information Security Officer. It is the custodian and executive officer of the first line of defense for the cyber security and information technology security and risk program for a given organization [1].

CnC – stands for command and control (server). Generally, a cloud-hosted server/ system often working in tandem with the usage of DGA-generated domains, the CnC is used by threat actors to control and manage infected and breached endpoints and servers (generally resident) on private networks [1].

DDoS – Distributed Denial of Service. It is generally used to represent a network-based attack that has the capability to overwhelm the target application or system with a flood of (TCP/UDP) traffic packets or even basic TCP acknowledgements like an ack [1].

SaaS – stands for software as a service. It is generally used to refer to the technique of delivering an application over the internet, as a (subscription) service. Most SaaS instances are multi-tenant, with virtual separation per tenant [1].

References

1. Badhwar (2021) The CISO's Next Frontier: AI, Post-Quantum Cryptography and Advanced Security Paradigms (Springer)

Further Read.ing

Bhattacharya N and Hay A (2021). Becoming a Next-Gen CISO: Leading from the Front (Webinar) https://www.infosecurity-magazine.com/webinars/nextgen-ciso/ Accessed March 11, 2021

Aleem A (2021) CISOs Must Lead from The Front on Security https://www.comparethecloud.net/articles/cisos-must-lead-from-the-front-on-security/ Accessed March 11, 2021

Kark K and Aguas T (2016) The new CISO: Leading the strategic security organization https://www2.deloitte.com/us/en/insights/deloitte-review/issue-19/ciso-next-generation-strategic-security-organization.htm Accessed March 11, 2021

McDermott S (2021) 2021: The Year of The Transformational CISO https://www.forbes.com/sites/forbestechcouncil/2021/03/01/2021-the-year-of-the-transformational-ciso, Accessed March 11, 2021

More CISOs on Corporate Boards

1 Preface

The Board of Directors (BoD) are the custodians of a company and of the interests of its shareholders. They also create policies for management and oversight of the company. Not only do they safeguard the company's best interests, but they are also responsible for detecting and mitigating any imminent threat that may do damage to a company, its brand or reputation, and to its shareholder value.

Cyber threats are the biggest driver of cyber risk – the most pervasive risk that businesses face these days, and it is thus an item that is generally on the top of the list of issues that concern the BoD of any company.

2 Let's Define Cyber Threats and Cyber Risk First

Cyber Threat is any information system related circumstance or event with the potential to adversely impact organizational operations, assets, or individuals, occurring via unauthorized access, destruction, disclosure, modification of information, denial of service or the potential for a threat-source to successfully exploit a particular information system vulnerability.

Cyber Risk is the risk of financial loss, disruption of service, or damage to the reputation of an organization from a security incident. Cyber risk can materialize through deliberate and unauthorized breaches of security to gain access to information systems; unintentional or accidental breaches of security; or operational IT risk due to systems integrity or other factors.

© The Author(s), under exclusive license to Springer Nature
Switzerland AG 2021
R. Badhwar, *The CISO's Transformation*,
https://doi.org/10.1007/978-3-030-81412-0_2

3 Making the Case

Most of the modern-day corporate boards are comprised of senior executives external to the company, including but not limited to current and/or former CEOs, CIOs, CFOs, Presidents and/or Chairmen with business, financial, legal, and operational expertise - but with very little expertise or knowledge in the matters of cyber threats and the massive cyber risk that a given company may carry.

Based on the several high-profile cyber breaches and incidents in the recent past (Target, Marriott, Yahoo, Home Depot, Equifax, Aramco, Sony, Capital One etc.) it has become abundantly clear that these breaches can bring a massive amount of business, financial and reputational risk and loss to a company, and that it may only take one successful attack to bring down a brand or reputation that may have taken years or even decades to build. Also, a lack of compliance with new local, state, or federal regulations and guidelines like NYDFS (New York Department of Financial Services), GDPR (General Data Protection Regulation), CCPA (California Consumer Privacy Act) can also cause massive reputational damage and open the possibility of huge fines from regulators. The list of various regulatory agencies with which a company must comply can be onerously long. In addition to the agencies just mentioned, there are also requirements from the SEC, DSS and FINRA, among others, depending upon the industry and location.

If an incident were to occur, an external CISO or a security subject matter expert (SME) on the board is best equipped to educate them regarding the imminent threat and business risk from the event and can help navigate and advise in this very stressful and complex situation regarding what steps to take to help establish a path to recovery. A security savvy board member can provide oversight and guidance on how to address an incident, which involves identifying the problem that caused the breach and forming a task force comprised of IT, business and security personnel; isolating and segmenting the damage and mitigating any residual risk; identifying and executing the remediation steps; sanitizing the IT systems and environment; developing a communication strategy, performing regulatory mandated breach disclosure within stipulated time, and last but not the least, engaging the cyber insurance provider. Such a board member could also help the board evaluate the overall effectiveness of the response.

To prevent a major security breach or incident from occurring or incurring a fine from a regulator (for non-compliance), the CISO on the board could be that trusted advisor that the board of directors need who is also an expert in the area of cyber security, can ask the right questions related to application security, and help to translate and communicate what and where the security risks are in the organization, can help decipher how mature the company's internal security organization is - are they focused on the right priorities, are they appropriately staffed and funded, do they have the right tools? A CISO on the board of directors then can help guide the company to make the case for the necessary security investments to help quantify and mitigate the risk from impending cyber threats by implementing the needed security controls, help navigate the various regulatory requirements landscape (NYDFS,

PCI DSS, CCPA and SEC disclosures), make smart risk management decisions, provide guidance about how to provide ongoing training about security, help develop an annual curriculum of cyber briefings and table top exercises, and also help align/translate security strategy with the company's business objectives.

4 The CISO Take

Gartner has rightfully predicted that 40% of Boards Will Have a Dedicated Cybersecurity Committee by 2025 [1]. The corporate boards need more external CISOs as directors to help the board understand and explore options to shore up the company against cyber security and regulatory risks; prioritize mitigation approaches, remediation options and capabilities; and validate the effectiveness and execution of a company's security program.

Also, per another prediction from Gartner, 75% of CEOs will be Personally Liable for Cyber-Physical Security Incidents by 2024 [2] and thus it is in the best interest of the CEOs who in many cases is also the chairman of company boards that they get a trusted CISO on the board to help them make sound decisions about how best to remediate or mitigate the cyber risk of the firm that they may be held liable for in case of a cyber incident or breach.

The CISOs can also help the board make the right decisions evaluating cyber and third-party risk while engaging in merger and acquisition (M&A) discussions.

5 Definitions

NYDFS – stands for New York state department of financial services. It supervises and regulates the activities of insurance companies, banking and other financial institutions in the state of NY.

PCI DSS – stands for payment card industry data security standard. It is generally meant to denote the set of security controls that must be implemented by businesses to protect credit card (CC) data. Businesses must maintain PCI DSS compliance to be able to process credit card financial transactions.

CCPA – stands for California consumer privacy act. It is California state regulation on consumer protection and privacy rights for California residents [3].

DSS – stands for Defense security service. DSS (now DCSA) performs personnel security monitoring and investigations, supervises industrial security, and conducts security education and awareness training for the military industrial complex.

CPRA – stands for California privacy rights act. It will amend and supersede CCPA once it goes in effect on January 1, 2023. It expands consumer privacy rights to align more closely with GDPR. [3]

References

1. Moore S (2021) Gartner Predicts 40% of Boards Will Have a Dedicated Cybersecurity Committee by 2025 https://www.gartner.com/en/newsroom/press-releases/2021-01-28-gartner-predicts-40%2D%2Dof-boards-will-have-a-dedicated- Accessed March 10, 2021
2. Moore S (2020) Gartner Predicts 75% of CEOs Will be Personally Liable for Cyber-Physical Security Incidents by 2024 https://www.gartner.com/en/newsroom/press-releases/2020-09-01-gartner-predicts-75%2D%2Dof-ceos-will-be-personally-liabl . Accessed Jan 5 2021.
3. Badhwar (2021) The CISO's Next Frontier: AI, Post-Quantum Cryptography and Advanced Security Paradigms (Springer)

Further Reading

Sridhara V (2020). CISOs: Quantifying cybersecurity for the board of directors - https://www.helpnetsecurity.com/2020/04/21/quantifying-cybersecurity/, Accessed Dec 24, 2020.

Fruhlinger J (2019). Does it matter who the CISO reports to? https://www.csoonline.com/article/3278020/does-it-matter-who-the-ciso-reports-to.html, Accessed Dec 24, 2020.

NYSE (2015). Cybersecurity in the board room. https://www.nyse.com/publicdocs/VERACODE_Survey_Report.pdf . Accessed March 11, 2021

Antova G (2020). Why Companies Need CISOs and CIOs as Board Members, https://www.securityweek.com/why-companies-need-cisos-and-cios-board-members, Accessed Dec 23, 2020.

Olyaei S, Thielemann K et al (2021). Predicts 2021: Cybersecurity Program Management and IT Risk Management. Accessed Feb 20, 2021. (Gartner)

Cyber Program Turnaround by New CISO

1 The Human Element

I have often heard new CISOs (and other executive leaders) say that they will turn a cyber security program around once they hire "their people" purging and reshuffling their new security teams to fill them with people with whom they have worked in previous positions. They talk about how they have to trust the people and thus bringing "their people" makes that easier and achievable. I wholeheartedly disagree with that statement and sentiment. New leaders will often perform a complete reset factored on their own personal comfort, but if it takes a bit of dis-comfort to start with the existing team, then so be it, because it is the right thing to do. I don't care who you are and which new company employs you, once you take over a security program, the existing team members ARE your people – it is okay not to trust them right away, because they have to earn your trust, and you have to earn theirs, but treating them as if they were from a now-defunct regime and replacing them with a new crew is not the smartest thing to do. I would engage in training and awareness campaigns to ensure that existing staff is well aware of any newer ideas that you want to preach and practice. Also, never blame the previous CISO about the state of the current program; always look forward by focusing on ideas and trying to build upon the strength of the previous program. Bring new ideas and tactical additions, but do not wipe the slate clean and start afresh with a whole new leadership team. If you want a quick turnaround of the program, then treat the existing team as YOUR PEOPLE. I promise, you will be successful.

This is one area where a security program is very similar to football. If you look at the football programs with remarkable turnarounds, one name comes to mind right away – Urban Meyer. Meyer successfully turned around multiple college football programs: Bowling Green, Utah, Florida, and then OSU, some as fast as 1 year. He has the same philosophy I am preaching here. Contrast that with the NFL coaches such as Bill Belichick, Bill Parcels, and Andy Reid, many of whom have

R. Badhwar, *The CISO's Transformation*, https://doi.org/10.1007/978-3-030-81412-0_3

taken many years to perform successful turnarounds. Urban did it multiple times over, and much faster.

2 Use of Security Frameworks

After taking over a new program, the new CISO must consider using security frameworks such as ISO 27001, NIST (800-53) or FFIEC (depending upon the business domain) to assess the IT eco system under their purview to understand the resident risk from a lack of proper security hygiene. Based on their assessment of the current state, they must drive the implementation of any necessary security controls, using a phased approach to move from the current, to an intermediate, and finally, to the desired target state of security by following these frameworks.

They must prioritize the remediation and mitigation activities to reduce the cumulative cyber risk by prioritizing the remediation of their (digital) internet-facing or other higher risk applications/systems and protecting the company 'crown jewels' using an approach that is in compliance with these frameworks, that will also pass regulatory muster (NYDFS, SEC/FINRA).

3 Adoption of a Cloud-Based Security Stack

Gone are the days when CISOs were able to secure their company by establishing a walled garden with an array of endpoint, network, and perimeter security tools, holding full control over the network egress and ingress of applications and systems hosted in on-premises data centers.

Instead of becoming a roadblock to the adoption and migration of IT systems and applications to the cloud, the new CISO must become an enabler of the secure adoption of the (public or private) cloud. They must proactively create design patterns reliant on cloud native or hybrid security tooling capabilities to ensure that the fundamental security posture used for on-premises environments is maintained on the cloud.

During this current phase of mass transition to the cloud, I would like to emphasize the importance of developing security design patterns for hybrid cloud scenarios. CISOs will have to contend with the reality of the hybrid cloud for a fairly long time, as on-premises applications and systems are moving to the cloud in a phased manner and will co-exist in both on-premise and public cloud environments for a substantial period.

The new CISO must lean into the innovation and agility of the cloud and implement and adopt modern cloud-native, cloud-hosted security tools. Cloud implementations can be done at a much faster pace than those of legacy on-premises security tools.

4   Zero Trust

Zero Trust is a security architecture and implementation paradigm that reduces enterprise risk by performing secure implementations in compliance with the principle that all assets inside and outside a perimeter firewall are not to be trusted. Access for users, devices, systems, and services must be controlled by applying the principle of least privilege with conditional access paradigm of continuous access validation.

The new CISO must preach the adoption of the 'Zero Trust' in conjunction with 'least access privilege' using a phased approach. Zero Trust is not a tool that can be deployed per se, it is a paradigm that must be followed as new systems are implemented and existing systems or environments are retooled and upgraded.

5   Seamless Biometric Authentication

CISOs must do their best to promote the elimination of passwords for network or application authentication. This can be done by replacing all legacy passwords with biometric authentication, enabled with physical traits such as facial, fingerprint, or retina recognition (depending upon the risk level). The hardware required for scanning these biometric traits has been perfected and made available for almost every laptop or device configuration, and companies like Apple (with Fingerprint and Face-ID) and Microsoft (with windows Hello) have already mainstreamed these capabilities by making them available natively within their operating systems.

6   Making Use of Threat Intelligence

Given the emergence of sophisticated malware and advanced persistent threat, CISOs must implement a threat intelligence platform to get real-time information and data from public and private intelligence sources to be informed of evolving or emerging threats or attacks. This would enable them to take proactive, protective defensive measures against possible attacks.

7   Active Board-Level Participation

New CISOs must actively engage with the company's board of directors and ensure that the cybersecurity program is adequately funded. They can use peer-based metrics to make a case for appropriate funding while gauging the board's cyber risk appetite. Aligning the cyber program's security posture with the board's perspective and insight on the company's business investments and priorities is crucial to the success of the new CISO.

The CISO must also solicit support from other C-level leaders (the CIO, CRO, and CTO) to ensure that the cybersecurity program is woven into the fabric of the company and not operating by itself on an island with depleted funding sources.

8   Effectiveness Testing

Generally, every corporate environment already has a security stack implemented. Generally, when new CISOs first arrive, many of them start replacing the existing stack with tools they are accustomed to using, on the assumption that such tools work better than those in the existing stack. The new CISO must take a systematic approach by immediately subjecting the newly inherited security stack to effectiveness testing. Such testing can be done with tools such as the Mandiant Security Validation tool (formerly Verodin). This would determine the capability of the stack to detect and protect from new threats and malware, picking up on the weakness of any ineffective legacy tools. This testing would highlight any existing gaps in protection, outdated configurations or rules, or duplicative tooling and capabilities. It would help sort the tools that should be kept from the ones that may need replacing.

9   The CISO Take

The average lifespan of a CISO at a given employer is touted to be less than 2 or 3 years. We have to work to change that. We have to stop resetting the program every couple of years with new leadership and new tools, which ultimately wastes time and precious resources. We should use fresh new ideas not to tear down existing security stacks, but to build and improve upon them. We should focus on teamwork, technological innovation, and employee development using the force of our technological and human resources to achieve the end goal of reducing and eliminating cyber risk, and build a reputation for excellence in customer and corporate security to help win the marketplace.

10   Definitions

CISO – stands for Chief information Security Officer. It is the custodian and executive officer of the first line of defense for the cyber security and information technology security and risk program for a given organization [1].

NIST – stands for National Institute of Standards and Technology. It is a non-regulatory US entity with the mission to promote innovation and industrial competitiveness.

NYDFS – stands for New York state department of financial services. It supervises and regulates the activities of insurance companies, banking and other financial institutions in the state of NY.

References

1. Badhwar (2021) The CISO's Next Frontier: AI, Post-Quantum Cryptography and Advanced Security Paradigms (Springer)

Further Reading

Shomo P (2019) Cybersecurity CISO Priorities for the Future https://www.darkreading.com/cloud/5-cybersecurity-ciso-priorities-for-the-future%2D%2D/a/d-id/1336325 Accessed March 11, 2021

Zwinggi A and Pineda M et al (2020) Why 2020 is a turning point for cybersecurity https://www.weforum.org/agenda/2020/01/what-are-the-cybersecurity-trends-for-2020/ Accessed March 11, 2021

McKinsey (2019) Perspectives on transforming cybersecurity https://www.mckinsey.com/~/media/McKinsey/McKinsey%20Solutions/Cyber%20Solutions/Perspectives%20on%20transforming%20cybersecurity/Transforming%20cybersecurity_March2019.ashx Accessed March 11, 2021

Ferguson D (2020) Top 5 First Strategic Steps for a New CISO https://securityboulevard.com/2020/05/top-5-first-strategic-steps-for-a-new-ciso/ Accessed March 11, 2021.

CISOs – The Next Step!

1 Introduction

The CISOs of today have risen from relative obscurity in a back office only a decade ago, to a quasi seat at the C-level table today. Their rise to prominence is attributable to their ability to protect firms from exponentially increasing cyber risk emanating from sophisticated malware, exfiltration of sensitive data, cyber-attacks, and Advanced Persistent Threat (APT). They also ensure compliance with various new government regulations on data security and privacy. But now they have to take the next step forward, emerging from the shadow of Risk and Information Technology to show real value beyond just delivering the information security needs for a firm.

According to Gartner, **"by 2023, 30% of a CISO's effectiveness will be directly measured on the ability to create value for the business."** [1]

It is high time that CISOs start creating value for businesses by helping build and deliver security services and security products.

2 Current State for Most Hands-on CISOs

CISOs are passionate about protecting the environments for which they are responsible. They spend all the time and resources they have at their disposal to develop and maintain comprehensive security programs for their companies. They go above and beyond to respond to various security and fraud incidents at any time of day or night; lead the delivery of security engineering innovations to keep ahead of insider and outsider cyber threats; manage seamless cyber security (IT) operations with no business or end-user impact; ensure timely (SOC1/SOC2) risk assessments and audits of internal applications and systems and external third-parties; and continue

© The Author(s), under exclusive license to Springer Nature
Switzerland AG 2021
R. Badhwar, *The CISO's Transformation*,
https://doi.org/10.1007/978-3-030-81412-0_4

to write, enhance, and evangelize security policy and standards for corporate compliance with local, state, and federal regulations.

To help companies win in the marketplace, they take part in business development activities, where they assert their (enhanced) capabilities in protecting customer and employee data, provide input for RFP and sales support wherever needed, and support customer retention efforts.

3   The Near-Future State

Most companies are getting out of hosting their applications and systems in their on-premises data centers. The advent of the cloud and the scale, agility, and cost savings it brings forth has led to the migration of most of the compute infrastructure to the cloud. What this means is that all the physical servers and appliances, the virtual server infrastructure (e.g., VMWare), all the storage filers (SAN, NAS etc.), all the data center networking equipment like switches and routers have moved either in whole or part to the cloud. This has also eliminated the need for many on-premises data center personnel and network engineers.

However, key points to remember here are that even if the compute and storage systems move to the cloud to make use of Infrastructure as a Service (IaaS) offerings from the cloud providers, it is still (a) the responsibility of the respective company CIO to manage the virtual private cloud (VPC) environments, the local networking and micro-segmentation, and the virtual storage and applications; and (b) the responsibility of the CISO to manage the data, network, web, and perimeter security, and Identity and Access Management in these cloud environments.

Thus, the mission of the CISO and the cyber security team remains unchanged: to maintain the confidentiality, integrity, and availability of all data and systems irrespective of where they may be hosted i.e., on the cloud or on-premises. There is, however, an opportunity for further optimization by giving the network engineering and operational responsibilities to the CISO. These have traditionally been part of the CIO/CTO teams, but should now be merged with the network security team under the leadership of the CISO to ensure all new network connectivity is engineered securely, provide better service, and reduce cost. The network security (or 'NetSec') team is already responsible for securing these network connections and are more than capable of performing the engineering as well.

This would make the CISO responsible for all cyber security in the cloud or on the premises and for the secure delivery of all network connectivity and all supporting networking infrastructure, from all physical and virtual office locations to the cloud datacenters.

4   The Not-So-Distant Future State

CISOs deserve their fair share and recognition as senior business and technology leaders. Although their work in securing a company's products and services brings critical value to customers, the fact that their work--generally confined to corporate cost centers--does not directly generate profit, means that they will not get their fair share. For that to happen, CISOs must pull their own weight in the corporate arena of profit generation, by being directly responsible for the creation of revenue-generating security products. Here are some ideas to consider.

4.1   Cybersecurity Product Development

There has been massive venture capital investment in the cyber security space. This has led to a proliferation of cyber security startups, often focusing on a single security product, leading to severe market segmentation of technical capabilities offered. Startups rarely offer one-stop shopping and a comprehensive suite of security products. To make matters worse, although some of these companies have implemented good, innovative products, their sole aim is to cash out by getting acquired by a bigger player. This trend has given me and some of my other CISOs pause, because when we select a security product from a vendor, and that vendor gets acquired, we then must deal with the very real prospect of the acquiring company diluting or stagnating future innovation of that product, potentially leading to the increase in company vulnerability to cyber-attacks. To add insult to injury, the change in licensing schemes from perpetual to subscription-based pricing puts us at the receiving end of rising costs, either on volume-based pricing or due to annual price increases. You may enter a deal with a lower subscription price than what you may have paid for a perpetual license but may be held hostage later with annual subscription price increases.

I believe it is high time that we started investing into in-house product development. CISOs know the security space the best and know the pulse of where they may be able to invest and develop a product that may best meet their needs and the needs of their sector. There are also opportunities to develop innovative products in response to our daily security challenges.

In the areas of cloud security, for example, we can develop a range of products, from those which secure automated orchestration for workloads in clouds and hybrid environments; to those which detect and mitigate fraud; authenticate via adaptive, step-up biometrics; make dynamic risk assessments; share threat intelligence; to those which secure financial data aggregation.

We need not reinvent the wheel by rewriting a new version of a SIEM or creating a new database, but we can certainly innovate, improve upon, update, and maintain the products and services we create in-house, a more effective strategy for dealing with increasing levels of cyber risk, rather than continuing to buy from segmented startups that may either fold or disappear into a bigger collective in a couple of years. Products developed in-house can also be monetized to develop new revenue streams.

4.2 Cybersecurity Services Development

Companies with mature cyber security programs and capabilities could position themselves to market and monetize their services externally. These types of services with potential for monetization include, but are not limited to, Cyber Security as a Service (CSaaS), Security Monitoring as a Service (MaaS), Threat Intelligence as a Service (TIaaS), and Fraud Detection as a Service (FDaaS).

4.3 Cyber Wellness

Cyber Wellness is a capability that can help an individual protect their social, personal, or financial identity from being compromised or stolen.

The wellness service could alert the individual if any of their personally identifiable information (PII) or data (such as their SSN, DOB, or financials) or their email or web-site login user-ids and password credentials are found within breach data on the web, in the hands of malicious entities, in hacking forums, or on the dark web.

The service could also monitor the individual's social media presence and alert in the event of an account takeover or any suspicious or malicious account behavior.

The wellness service could also provide step-by-step guidance on what to do in the event of a personal account breach or an identity theft, with protection measures and schemes to engage law enforcement agencies and insurance entities, and to take other steps required by an individual to regain control over their identity or their compromised accounts.

These services could be sold as an add-on product to augment existing relationships with a consumer. E.g., in the financial services space, a cyber-wellness service could be provided for free along with the financial wellness services already provided, then later once the user recognizes the value proposition of the same, this service could be used to retain a customer or a small monthly charge could be added for premium capabilities like dark-web scanning.

4.4 Cyber Insurance Certification and Attestation

Given the exponential rise of sophisticated malware, ransomware and cyber-attacks worldwide, gone are the days where one could buy cyber insurance by filling out a one-page form.

The last five years has seen cyber insurance claims filed to the tune of hundreds of millions of dollars leading to mounting losses for the cyber insurance providers [3]. To maintain the solvency and viability of the cyber insurance business, the insurance underwriters need the capability to either dynamically assess and quantify the cyber risk resident within a given organization, or someone to certify and attest that the needed security controls to prevent malware and ransomware have indeed been implemented, before they can underwrite a policy for these entities.

The CISOs and the cybersecurity team with advanced cyber programs and expertise in implementing security controls can stand up a security certification and attestation service that can analyze and review the IT ecosystems of prospective customers and perform the said certification and attestation.

There are two business opportunities here – first is to establish a partnership with insurance providers and be their designated certification and attestation provider, second to provide assessment services to other businesses to help them pre assess their environments for security hygiene so that they can make the necessary security control implementations to be able to purchase a cyber insurance policy.

CISOs of financial services companies with exiting relationships with other large client companies can offer this capability as an additional value-add service.

4.5   How Can This Be Delivered?

Successful delivery of these new security product and service revenue streams hinges upon the leadership of next generation CISOs, here defined as hands-on, strategic out-of-the-box thinkers who solve complex security problems and bring innovation to security product development. They should be able to make the business case to the board of directors to invest in product development, and lead architecture and subsequent delivery of product and service ideas to fruition.

5   The CISO Take

Most of the CISOs I know are hard-working highly technical professionals full of ideas. Not only are they well-versed in the engineering aspects of the various security tools but they also have years of hands-on experience implementing, configuring, and using security products and technologies. CISOs are thus ideally suited to put their backgrounds to use to create exciting cyber security products and services.

Historically speaking the CISOs were never consulted in the selection and implementation of the application or infrastructure portfolios, but the move to the cloud has highlighted the intrinsic need of application and infrastructure security to be woven into the fabric of the entire ecosystem rather than something that can be latched on later (as in the past). Thus, the CISOs are ideally suited for and will eventually become the custodians of the company applications, systems and the technology networking stack irrespective of whether the hosting solution is in the cloud or on-premises, as the application engineering and operational needs will merge with that of securing the same.

To make their companies more secure and add value to the role of the CISO, I challenge CISOs to be leaders and not followers and to be strategic and not tactical, by proactively designing and securing the applications correctly the first time while they are being implemented rather than after the fact when weaknesses are discovered or breaches have occurred. Help your fellow (cyber) security professional, and in-turn seek help when you need it from the security collective. I am passionate in my belief that the CISOs can create and deliver additional value for the enterprise and the business.

6 Definitions

APT – stands for Advanced Persistent Threat. It is used to describe a campaign of attacks by persistent sophisticated threat actors whose intent is to gain long-term residence or presence on the network of the target. The list of malicious activities includes but is not limited to stealing intellectual property or company sensitive data, sabotaging key network segments or systems, installing and operating backdoors to communicate with CnC servers, and conducting complete site takeovers. These attacks are complex, targeted, well-resourced and funded, and are generally conducted by nation states or other criminal organizations.

CnC – stands for command and control (server). It is generally a cloud-hosted server/system using DGA-generated domains used by threat actors to control and manage infected and breached endpoints and servers (generally resident) on private networks. [4]

DGA – stands for a Domain Generation Algorithm. It is a program that uses an algorithm to generate a list of domain names that can be used by malware (or an insider threat) for the sites (hosting a CnC server) that give it instructions, and also to quickly switch the domains that they're using for the attacks if a malicious domain is blocked by the security teams.

IaaS – stands for Infrastructure as a Service. It is a cloud computing capability by which a cloud services provider enables access to computing resources such as virtual servers, storage, networking, and many other cloud-native security services such as firewalls, HSM, and WAF. These are used by users or corporations to host their private applications and systems within a cloud computing provider's infrastructure.

PII – stands for Personally Identifiable Information. Any representation of information that permits the identity of an individual to be reasonably inferred by either direct or indirect means. Further, PII is defined as information which: (i) directly identifies an individual (e.g., name, address, social security number or other identifying number or code, telephone number, or email address) or (ii) an agency intends to identify specific individuals in conjunction with other data elements, i.e., indirect identification. [2]

References

1. Wasko B (2020) How Security and Risk Leaders Can Prepare for Reduced Budgets. Available via Gartner. https://www.gartner.com/smarterwithgartner/how-security-and-risk-leaders-can-prepare-for-reduced-budgets/ . Accessed Dec 24, 2020.
2. US Department of Labor. Guidance on the Protection of Personal Identifiable Information. https://www.dol.gov/general/ppii . Accessed Dec 24, 2020.
3. Johansmeyer T (2021) Cybersecurity Insurance Has a Big Problem https://hbr.org/2021/01/cybersecurity-insurance-has-a-big-problem Accessed Feb 24, 2020
4. Badhwar (2021) The CISO's Next Frontier: AI, Post-Quantum Cryptography and Advanced Security Paradigms (Springer)

Further Reading

Ritchey D (2020) The Changing Role of the CISO. In: Security magazine (Feb 2020) - https://www.securitymagazine.com/articles/91653-the-changing-role-of-the-ciso. Accessed July 5, 2020.
Fazzini K (2018) Companies Unleash CISOs from Ties to Tech Chiefs. The Wall Street Journal (24 April 2018) https://www.wsj.com/articles/companies-cut-ciso-reporting-ties-with-technology-1524515201. Accessed 5 July, 2020.
Bisson D (2019) Leadership Through Security: The Changing Role of the CISO. Available via Tripwire: The State of Security https://www.tripwire.com/state-of-security/security-awareness/leadership-through-security-changing-role-ciso/. Accessed 5 July, 2020.
Rosario K (2020) Ransomware Exposure Is Causing Cyber Insurance Costs to Skyrocket https://tgsinsurance.com/news/cyber/ransomware-exposure-is-causing-cyber-insurance-costs-to-skyrocket/
Kreitzberg D (2020) Ransomware Cyber Insurance Claim Amounts Skyrocket https://designedprivacy.com/ransomware-cyber-insurance-claim-amounts-skyrocket/

CISO Maturity Model

1 Introduction

The CISO role has become multi-faceted: the ability to manage up, working effectively with executive leadership and boards of directors; make a case for appropriate funding for the cyber security program; to manage down, building and maintaining a strong security team, hiring strong talent by leaving no stone of potential unturned; to work cross-functionally with IT and Risk peers; to help the firm win the market place by aiding business development; and, most importantly, to have the technological background for wise decision-making for appropriate cyber risk remediation while dealing with a complex incident, or for mergers and acquisitions.

Seasoned CISOs are familiar with security engineering and operations, security architecture, incident response, fraud detection, cyber risk assessment, vulnerability management, and business continuity management to assess the current deployments and make the necessary upgrades wherever required. They have capability to deal with legacy and existing threats, but can also plan for the future, and build protections against the advanced next-generation threats already here or just on the horizon.

2 The Maturity Model

The CISO is not a monolithic entity. In fact, most of us perform a role that requires both business and technology acumen. Many of us specialize in security technologies and some of us specialize in business knowledge, but almost all of us have had at least some exposure to both these workstreams. Many of us often come out of niche security backgrounds, whether corporate, government, or military. Perhaps our previous work focused on a single security area, whether engineering,

© The Author(s), under exclusive license to Springer Nature
Switzerland AG 2021
R. Badhwar, *The CISO's Transformation*,
https://doi.org/10.1007/978-3-030-81412-0_5

architecture, or operations, or incident management and response, or cyber risk assessment and management, or it focused on physical security and compliance with local, state of federal security, privacy, and compliance regulations.

This chapter presents a new CISO maturity model which uses a 9 Box approach to classify:

(a) The various CISO levels and known types
(b) The journey from an entry level CISO to that of an executive CISO.

The Fig. 1 below depicts the model and additional details for each level.

The Fig. 1 not only shows the various levels of a CISO but also the path of progression of a CISO from one level to another. These are discussed in greater details within the technical, business and hybrid tracks below.

CISO Maturity Model (CMM)

Business Acumen ↑	Sales CISO (3)	CSO (7)	Executive CISO (9)
	• Customer/Client facing • Uses security and marketing skills • Makes the cases for security • Revenue Generator • Can translate customer requirements into implementation level details and vice-versa. • Attends conferences to represent the business or product team • Has a business degree (e.g. MBA)	• Can be customer facing • Manages Fraud and compliance • Manages EC physical security • Manages Business Resilience • Product Security • Not hands on Security Technologist • Has a strong technical second • Strong communicator • Leadership on regulatory issues	• Business Enabler and Leader • Helps with M&A. Product Creator • Board and EC confidant • Monetizes Security Services • Runs integrated Security and IT operations and infrastructure • Mature Cyber Practice • Retains top talent. • Full cloud enablement • Handles all regulatory needs
	BISO (2)	**Core CISO (6)**	**High Impact CISO (8)**
	• Recommends security solutions • Balances cyber vs business risk • Good relationship with business • Mitigates Business Fraud • Extension of the CISO team • Conveys security requirements to CISO team • Security Evangelist • Has audit or risk certifications	• Built business relationships • Learned the business over the years • Earned the business trust • Can assume business risk • Has matured the IT Security shop • Uses managed services • Has good talent management ability • Collaborates with IT and Risk • Mature Incident Response team • Conducts cyber drills	• Good knowledge of the business • Understands business needs • Cyber risk is quantified • Help business win the market • Hands on Security technologist • Great leader and motivator • Runs the First line of defence • Automation in security operations • Incorporates IAM with InfoSec • Delegates to leadership team
	Entry Level CISO (1)	**Effective CISO (4)**	**Security Controls CISO (5)**
	• Basic business knowledge • Attends security risk meetings • Basic understand of Fraud risk • Very IT & Access controls focused • Technical, Tactical & Reactive • Has many security certifications • Favours manual approaches • New in the org • Tendency to micro manage	• Improved knowledge of business risk • Factors business impacts while making security decisions • Uses security frameworks • Maintains security certifications • Detect and Respond • Defend and Protect • Proactive. Has an annual plan • Mature Incident Response	• Well engaged with the business • Helps with RFIs and RFPs • Helps with regulatory needs • Strategic and Innovative • Has key certifications only • Security presentations to board • Security target state and roadmap • Cost optimized • Security Engineering & Operations

Cybersecurity Expertise →

Fig. 1 CISO Maturity Model (CMM)

2.1   The Technical Track

CISOs generally follow two tracks – a technical track or a business track. Technical CISOs tend to focus on security controls implementations and regulatory compliance. Business-facing CISOs spend most of their time showcasing the sound security state of a company or a product to help with sale of products or services to prospective customers and clients. Only a small percentage of CISOs in the industry can do both (highlighted in this chapter as the hybrid track).

I came up the food chain as a technologist, shaped by my experience in identity management and (security) systems engineering and subsequent specialization in (post-quantum) cryptography, artificial intelligence and machine learning, and cloud security and zero trust. During the early part of my Security leadership journey, I had various security (e.g., CISSP), network (e.g., CCDA) and IT (e.g., ITIL) certifications, but now only carry the core cybersecurity certifications (CEH, CISSP) but have also acquired key business certifications to help aid with regulatory compliance (e.g., Finra Series 99). However, I am also proud of the work I have done to help my employers win the marketplace by either helping with business proposals and contract bids or making the case for the good state of the cybersecurity program citing our ability to maintain the confidentiality and integrity of our customer data from all threat vectors, make a similar case to regulators to assert compliance with various local, state or federal regulations and policies.

For the technical track, the path of progression is –

Level 1 - > Level 4 - > Level 5 - > Level 8 - > Level 9.

Level 1 (L1 CISO)

The level 1 (L1) is that of an entry-level CISO. This describes someone who has at least 6–8 years of experience dealing in information security, business security, risk management or regulatory work.

The L1 CISO does not have much business domain knowledge and is very IT and Access control focused. Most of the decisions made are tactical in nature as a direct reaction to situations and cyber incidents.

The L1 CISO generally is up to date on all the needed security certifications (like CISSP, OSCP etc.), or even networking certifications like (CCNP or CCIE) that allow them to stay current with security and technology implementations.

Generally, a L1 CISO is in charge of a security program for a smaller organization with simpler IT infrastructure and often has the internal title of IT or Security Director. These CISOs are often new to the organization and are the lowest compensated CISOs in the industry.

These CISOs are generally employed by small-mid size firms and have team sizes of 10-25 engineers, and report into CIOs or Technology heads.

Level 4 (L4 CISO)

The Level 4 (L4) CISO at least has 10 years of cybersecurity experience, generally with good technical security and IT skills. They also have over a shorter time period developed knowledge of at least one business sector, such as insurance, banking, pharmaceuticals, or manufacturing.

The L4s also have improved knowledge of the regulatory requirements that their firm must comply with. They have also begun automating the access management and incident processes and have fully flushed out tactical cybersecurity and incident response improvement plans.

The L4s still carry security certifications but only in domains where a certification is required for regulatory compliance or to maintain a security clearance or eligibility.

These CISOs are employed by mid-size firms, often have the internal title of Senior (Security) Director or AVP, have team sizes of 25-50 engineers, and generally report into CIOs or CROs.

Level 5 (L5 CISO)

The very technical L5 CISO focuses on the implementation of security controls, following a security control framework such as NIST 800-53 or ISO 27001.

While their focus is not the business, these CISOs do get some time with the company's senior leadership and the board of directors, making quarterly presentations to their company's Executive Committee and annual presentations to the board of directors.

These CISOs generally establish a current, intermediate and future state for a security program, have automated most of the repeatable process, have started an implementation of security paradigms like Zero Trust and have a good handle on security operations and transformation costs.

The L5's may still carry a core security certification (e.g., CISSP or ISSAP) or two, but their business and security experience provide more value than any security certification would.

These CISOs are generally employed by mid-large firms, often have the internal title of Vice President, and have team sizes of 50+ engineers, and may report into CIO, CROs or CLOs.

2.2 The Business Track

Many CISOs are on the business track and use their security knowledge and business acumen to bolster the sales and marketing operations of their employers. CISOs in this category also have a very good understanding of the business operations and the specific cyber and third-party risks to which the business or line of business

(LOB) may be exposed. Apart from a technical background, many of these CISOs have a business degree or legal background.

For the business track the path of progression is –

Level 1 - > Level 2 - > Level 3 - > Level 6.

Level 2 (L2 CISO)

An L2 CISO role generally manifests as a business information security officer (BISO). While in this role, the L2 CISO (or BISO) generally reports to and works closely with the global corporate CISO to help to translate security standards and requirements to the business and communicate any business constraints or exceptions back to the security team. The BISO also helps to prioritize the security control implementation, vulnerability management and application remediation activities in a manner that is least intrusive and non-impacting to business operations for a given line of business (LOB), thereby enabling an appropriate balance between information security requirements and smooth business operations.

Many large corporations with different lines of business (LOBs) have BISOs as heads of cybersecurity for each LOB, reporting into the global or corporate CISO. These BISOs generally do not run the security operations per se, but rather focus on risk management, coordinating all cybersecurity engineering, operations and implementations specific to the LOB with the centralized CISO team. Many BISOs have internal titles of Director.

The BISOs generally do not have core security certifications and may focus more on audit (CISA) or security management (CISM) type certifications.

Generally, BISO compensation is not on par with that of the global CISO. The BISO position can be a stepping stone to the global CISO or CSO role.

Level 3 (L3 CISO)

A Level 3 CISO is generally a client and customer facing role. Their primary mission is to aid the sales and marketing teams sell the product by citing the good state of the application security features of the company's products or services. They also take part in hackathons, open-source community, RFC/RFI development and responses, and national and international governance bodies. They also help interact with schools and universities to attract cybersecurity talent for their firms. Many L3 CISOs also interact with regulators, and federal and state government engagements, or lobby on behalf of the company to preserve their interests.

In addition to Security and IT backgrounds, the L3 CISOs may have business degrees (e.g., MBA) or backgrounds.

These CISOs are generally employed by mid-large product firms, have internal titles of AVP, and generally serve in a matrixed organization reporting to the CIO or CTO.

Level 6 (Core CISO)

A Level 6 (Core) CISO is really a jack of all security-related trades for mid-sized firms. They generally have long(er) tenures at a given firm and develop good business knowledge to augment their cyber security expertise, with an overall cyber security experience of at least 12 years.

These CISOs are generally employed at Fortune 500 firms, and other mid-sized firms, have internal titles of VP, and generally report into CIOs.

2.3 The Hybrid Track

These CISOs are the 'been there done that' type. They are generally long tenured and have at least 15–20 years of experience covering multiple business sectors (e.g., banking, insurance, retirement, investment management, defense).

For the hybrid track the path of progression is –

Level 7 - > Level 9.
Level 8 - > Level 9.

Level 7 (CSO)

A level 7 CISO (CSO) is a senior security executive with at least 20 years of experience. In the past, this genre of CISO/CSOs mostly had physical security backgrounds originating in the military or other defense-related security services. This has become of late a growth or promotion path for many L6 or L5 CISOs.

Apart from being responsible and accountable for Physical security for all sites and locations for a given firm, they are generally accountable for managing and mitigating all fraud and compliance issues. They also manage the business resilience office (BRO) and business continuity management (BCM) functions.

These CSOs are strong communicators and have great leadership skills but are not the most technical and generally have a strong second or deputy CISO to manage security engineering and operations while they play an external facing role. They are highly compensated and spend at least 40–50% of their time on the road and are generally employed by Fortune 250 companies, have internal titles of SVP, and may report into the CEO or CIO.

Level 8 (High-Impact CISO)

These are the highly technical, hands-on CISOs who have at least 20 years of experience and are super passionate about their job and role. Their technical experience and business knowledge also spans multiple business sectors. Many of these CISOs (can) also perform CTO roles.

Most of these CISOs are still hands on and can do almost any task their direct reports can do. Not only are they skilled in security engineering and operations but they are also adept at writing security policy and standards.

The security programs under the tutelage of these CISOs are mature, relying on paradigms like Zero Trust and NIST (800-53)-based frameworks for security control implementations.

These CISOs understand the security programs are cost centers and thus use their experience and knowledge to automate all manual tasks. They also make the case for security products and services development to generate revenue. These CISOs are compensated better than most of the lower level (L1-L6) CISOs, are generally employed by Fortune 250 companies, have internal titles of SVP, and may report into CIOs.

Level 9 (Executive CISO)

These industry icons and consummate security technologists are few and far between, with more than 25 years of cyber security and business experience.

They have good relationships with their company's executive leaders and the board of directors. They are also trusted partners in mergers and acquisitions (M&A).

These CISOs are great security leaders but have also created and monetized security products and services. These CISO also attract (and retain) great cybersecurity talent to build a great (although expensive) cybersecurity program.

Given the recent evolution of cybersecurity and the long-standing role of physical security, these have generally been two separate roles, but there are compelling reasons to put both cyber and physical security under the aegis of the leader who can oversee both aspects of security. This requires the recognition that a company cannot maintain cyber security without physical security, and vice-versa. These CISOs generally run their cyber security programs that are inclusive of and integrated with Physical security and Business continuity management programs.

Given the exponential increase in cyber risk and sophisticated attacks globally, another trend that has emerged in the industry is the integration of all company application and networking infrastructure with the cyber security operations under the leadership of the trusted (L9) CISO. These CISOs are the highest compensated security persons in the industry, on par with other C-level executives like CFOs and CIOs, are generally employed by Fortune 100 companies, have internal titles of EVP, and report to the CEO or the board of directors.

3 The CISO Take

The CISO maturity model (CMM) depicts the dramatic developments in the CISO role over the past decade, leading to the creation of various sub categorizations and specializations for the role defined here.

To some becoming a CISO may be a career milestone, but the CISO community further has its own career growth path given the length and breadth of the role, the complexity of the IT ecosystems they protect, and the size of the firms and the local/ global nature of the firms they are employed by.

Hopefully this model will help the CISO community chart their progression to the next level in their career.

4   Definitions

CISO – stands for Chief information Security Officer. It is the custodian and executive officer of the first line of defense for the cyber security and information technology security and risk program for a given organization [1].

CISSP – stands for Certified Information Systems Security Professional. It is a core and premier cyber security certification.

CEH – stands for certified ethical hacker. It is an ethical hacking certification.

OSCP – stands for Offensive Security Certified Professional. It is a premier offensive security certification.

NIST – stands for National Institute of Standards and Technology. It is a non-regulatory US entity with the mission to promote innovation and industrial competitiveness.

ISO 27001 – stands for International Organization for Standardization. It is a standard that provides instructions on how to manage an information security program, detailing requirements for program establishment, implementation, and maintenance.

References

1. Badhwar (2021) The CISO's Next Frontier: AI, Post-Quantum Cryptography and Advanced Security Paradigms (Springer)

Further Reading

Aguas T, Kark K (2016) The new CISO Leading the strategic security organization. https://www2.deloitte.com/content/dam/insights/us/articles/ciso-next-generation-strategic-security-organization/DR19_TheNewCISO.pdf. Accessed 20 Feb 2021

Babel T (2019) Is your CISO really C-Level? https://pentestmag.com/is-your-ciso-really-c-level/. Accessed 20 Feb 2021

Pollard J, Budge J, et al (2020) The Future of The CISO — Six Types of Security Leaders. https://go.forrester.com/blogs/the-future-of-the-ciso-six-types-of-security-leaders/. Accessed 20 Feb 2021

Schwartz S (2020) 6 types of CISO and the companies they thrive in https://www.ciodive.com/news/forrester-chief-information-security-officer-cyber/585682/. Accessed 20 Feb 2021

Schulman J (2015) 7 Types of CISOs. https://www.linkedin.com/pulse/7-types-cisos-jay-schulman/ . Accessed 20 Feb 2021

Hayslip G (2018) Will the real CISO please stand up? https://www.linkedin.com/pulse/real-ciso-please-stand-up-gary-hayslip-cissp-/. Accessed 20 Feb 2021

CISO Commentary on Some Emerging and Disruptive Technologies

1 Introduction

Early in 2020 before the pandemic, I attended a security conference held in NYC, as a panelist. The topic of the panel discussion was "Emerging and Disruptive Technologies."

Included in the discussion were these specific emerging and/or disruptive technologies that may have an impact on cyber security:

(a) Blockchain
(b) Artificial Intelligence and Machine Learning
(c) Hyper converged compute and storage
(d) Zero Trust with micro-segmentation
(e) Advanced Encryption
(f) Internet of things (IOT)
(g) Memory-Driven Computing
(h) Quantum Computing
(i) Quantum Cryptography
(j) Robotic Process Automation (RPA)
(k) Digital Me

These were some of the security-related questions raised about these technologies:

1. What is the impact of new technologies on cybersecurity? How can these technologies aid us and protect us (e.g., AI in cybersecurity)?
2. At the same time, what vulnerabilities do they present? What new tools do they provide to hackers?
3. Do new areas such as homomorphic encryption, quantum encryption, cryptography, and robotic process automation provide increased protection but also present an increased likelihood of more vulnerabilities?

© The Author(s), under exclusive license to Springer Nature
Switzerland AG 2021
R. Badhwar, *The CISO's Transformation*,
https://doi.org/10.1007/978-3-030-81412-0_6

2 Security Commentary

Please find below my very brief commentary on the technologies listed above. Given that these are important topics with implications on cyber security, they have been covered in a far greater detail within other sections in my previous more technical book [2], but here are the comments I shared with some of the attendees, in an attempt to provide a view on the leadership aspect of the CISO role.

Most security technologists would agree with me when I say that the mission of all security teams has always been to be an enabler and sustainer of business rather than a roadblock. All the new emerging and disruptive technologies bring expanded capabilities to aid the businesses, but sometime also present some challenges from a security perspective. Security technologists always find a way to either remediate the vulnerabilities or implement mitigating controls to minimize or transfer the risk. Some details are shared below:

1. While it is a well-documented fact that **blockchain** has created a new ecosystem for micro-payments and crypto-currency transactions and has found widespread use in supply chain management, accounting, smart contracts, voting, stock exchange, insurance, shipping and peer-to-peer global transactions, it has also been plagued by various security issues like the "51% Attack," "Sybil Attack," "Penny-Flooding Attack," "Penny-Spend attack," "Transaction flooding," "Time-jacking attack," "Eclipse attack," "Steganographic attack," and "Silkroad attack." Security technologists around the world have collaborated to find many remediations, patches and mitigation techniques to keep this ecosystem safe for use, but continuous evaluation needs to be done to ensure that all new vulnerabilities are proactively patched.

2. The adoption of **Artificial Intelligence and Machine Learning** has the potential to revolutionize every industry (software, service, manufacturing, medical, finance, banking, etc.), and through developments such as the Internet of Things (IOT), almost every aspect of life as we know it today. Machine Learning and supervised AI are currently only as good as the training datasets and thus suffer from false positives (from a security perspective). Also, unsupervised AI, if left unmanaged or without a code of ethics, runs the risk of evolutionary computation induced drift and the potential lack of algorithmic transparency and accountability.

3. **Zero Trust** is a security architecture and implementation paradigm that reduces enterprise risk by performing secure implementations in compliance with the principal that all assets inside and outside a perimeter firewall are not to be trusted and thus access control for users, devices, systems and services must be provided using least privilege. These implementations do have the tendency to lead to additional infrastructural and application complexity, and increased costs.

4. **Hyperconverged storage and compute** provide various advantages of better scalability and theoretical simplicity but suffer from the disadvantages of high-power consumption due to high equipment density, higher and/or unmanaged licensing costs and lack of compatibility with other cloud and/or on-premises

infrastructures. Hyperconverged infrastructure (HCI) may also conflict with the security concepts of Zero trust unless built into the HCI.

5. The advent of quantum computing and its supposed (future state) capability to break all encryption based on computational difficulty has raised data security and privacy concerns and has put renewed focus on **advanced encryption**. Cryptographers and other security technologists are proactively working to improve existing cryptographic mechanisms, and also to find alternative mechanisms of encryption resistant to attacks from quantum computers. Creating a Diffie-Hellman replacement with forward secrecy using the properties of super-singular elliptic curves is an EXISTING cryptographic scheme enhancement. Some of the possible NEW schemes are lattice-based cryptography, code-based and hash-based cryptography, and multi-variate cryptography.

6. **IOT (internet of things)** has created an automated, cost effective way to enable real-time intercommunication between users and devices among many other things and has helped provide access to information that enables multiple business and consumer friendly use cases. On the flip side, IOT also presents many data security and privacy issues – these can be mitigated by using security paradigms like Network segmentation (by putting the IOT devices on a segmented network), Network Access Control (by doing device based authentication and using 802.1X authentication), by disabling Bluetooth and blocking their capability to connect to unauthorized wireless networks, Auto detecting and inventorying all IOT devices within CMDB, ensuring that IOT devices are patched for vulnerabilities just like other computing devices, and ensuring that they use strong (knowledge and token based) authentication paradigms.

7. **Memory-Driven Computing** sets itself apart by giving every processor in a system access to a giant shared pool of memory—a sharp departure from today's systems where a relatively small amount of memory is tethered to each processor. While this may bring in enormous performance optimizations, this certainly raises data security concerns [1].

8. **Quantum computing** applies the principles of quantum mechanics to computers. The difference between conventional and quantum computing models is that while an N bit register in a conventional computer can store only one of N binary configurations at any given time, an N qubit register can store all the N states simultaneously. This makes a quantum computer very powerful and can cause an exponential increase in computing power. It is the belief of some that in a post-quantum computing era, all the encryption algorithms that are based on computational difficulty will fail, and other encryption schemes (like quantum encryption) may be the lone ones left standing, raising many data security and preservation of data confidentiality concerns. I personally think that both computational and quantum-based encryption algorithms would find their rightful place in the post-quantum computing target state.

9. **Quantum Cryptography** offers a (theoretically) secure solution to the issue of secure key exchange that may plague (mostly) symmetrical and (to some extent) asymmetrical cryptosystems. It provides some enhanced capability to detect man-in-the-middle (MITM) attacks. It also limits exposure to certain weaknesses

that may exist in conventional cryptosystems due to its ability to restrict the capability to copy data encoded in a quantum state.

10. **Homomorphic encryption** allows computations to be carried out directly on encrypted data. These computations generate a result which is the same as if the computations were done on unencrypted data or plaintext. This form of encryption suffers from slow performance and currently is only supported for a limited number of mathematical operations.

11. **Robotic Process Automation** (aka RPA or RPA bots) performs certain high volume, manual, and repeatable tasks that were previously performed by humans (e.g., call center agents and back-office personnel) in the IT industry. Over the last five to seven years, there has been significant improvement in the capability of these RPA bots funneled by the investment in this technology area by both big industry players and startups. There are generally two types of RPA bots prevalent in the industry at the current time – attended and unattended bots. This technology brings an undoubtable value proposition to the IT industry for multiple use cases (improving productivity, efficiency, agility and customer service). However, just as new risks arise with the adoption of any other disruptive and emerging technology, there must be more rigorous analysis, identification, remediation and mitigation of any RPA-related security risks.

12. **Digital me** enables the capability to create a digital (or twin) representation that can be used to represent an individual in both physical and digital space. The 2020/21 pandemic has further highlighted this by enabling the creation of digital personas of humans to safely share their health profile or enable social distancing without compromising their ability to engage in meaningful dialog. This technology is moving beyond text and images into fully formed voice enabled holographic images that can represent an individual using a digital twin. Obviously, this capability needs to be properly secured due to the fear of someone's digital twin/identity being stolen and then subsequently used to impersonate an individual for financial gain or for conducting other malicious activities.

3   The CISO Take

Modern CISOs are expected to be able to review new technologies and determine their impacts, if any, on the state of the cyber and information security for a given enterprise.

The release of many newer technologies (e.g., blockchain, IOT, and RPA) without the needed hardening and security controls has led to many breaches. This should serve as a reminder about the need to secure these technologies and penetration test them before they are made generally available.

CISOs have to be leaders in this space, not only to perform impact analysis, but to shape the conversation in a way so that the cyber security aspects are front and center of conversations prior to and during the selection and implementation of a given new technology, rather than a mere post-implementation afterthought.

4 Definitions

Blockchain – is an immutable and distributed digital ledger. The records (blocks) are linked to each other using a Merkle tree - where each block contains a cryptographic hash (e.g., SHA2) of the previous block, a timestamp and ledger (transaction) data [2].

Bot – is a short form for robot. It has the capability to perform certain high volume, manual, and repeatable tasks that were previously performed by humans. Bots perform these tasks much faster than humans [2].

CISO – stands for Chief information Security Officer. It is the custodian and executive officer of the first line of defense for the cyber security and information technology security and risk program for a given organization [2].

Cryptocurrency – is digital (or virtual) currency built using blockchain technology that can be used to pay for goods and services (just like the paper currency) [2].

IOT – stands for internet of things. It is used to describe a system where ubiquitous sensors and smart devices are continuously connected to the internet.

MITM – stands for man-in-the-middle. It is a type of cyber-attack where an attacker hijacks a secure encrypted connection between a client and server.

References

1. Hewlett Packard Enterprise Blog Staff Writer (2017) Memory-Driven Computing Explained. https://news.hpe.com/memory-driven-computing-explained/. Accessed 24 Dec 2020
2. Badhwar (2021) The CISO's Next Frontier: AI, Post-Quantum Cryptography and Advanced Security Paradigms (Springer)

Further Reading

Wikipedia. Quantum Cryptography. https://en.wikipedia.org/wiki/Quantum_cryptography. Accessed 24 Dec 2020

Bednarz A (2019) What is hyperconvergence? In: Network World. https://www.networkworld.com/article/3207567/what-is-hyperconvergence.html. Accessed 24 Dec 2020

Kaspersky (2017) Internet of Things Security Threats. In: Kapersky Home Security Resource Center. https://www.kaspersky.com/resource-center/threats/internet-of-things-security-risks. Accessed 24 Dec 2020

Wallen J (2017) Five nightmarish attacks that show the risks of IoT security. https://www.zdnet.com/article/5-nightmarish-attacks-that-show-the-risks-of-iot-security/. In: ZDNet Special Feature: Cybersecurity in an IOT and Mobile World. Accessed 19 Jan 2021

Hippold S (2019) How Digital Twins Simplify the IoT https://www.gartner.com/smarterwithgartner/how-digital-twins-simplify-the-iot/

Schatz J (2019) Considering RPA? Make sure you understand the security implications. https://gcn.com/articles/2019/12/18/rpa-security.aspx Accessed 19 Jan 2021

Gartner (2020) Gartner Identifies Five Emerging Trends That Will Drive Technology Innovation for the Next Decade https://www.gartner.com/en/newsroom/press-releases/2020-08-18-gartner-identifies-five-emerging-trends-that-will-drive-technology-innovation-for-the-next-decade

Wang Z and Ma W (2021) Digital Me: Toward Digitalizing Everybody in the World https://www.microsoft.com/en-us/research/project/digital-me/

See Something, Do Something!

1 Genesis

The exponential increase in the cyber threats and attacks from malicious entities, insider threat, advanced persistent threat and malware, have also led to an equally large increase in the effort to protect our sensitive data from these threats leading to the creation of dedicated cyber security and risk programs at most firms.

CISOs have risen to prominence from relative obscurity to create sophisticated programs using a plethora of tools that encompass various security domains like endpoint security, network security, perimeter security, data security, email security, application security and cloud security. They have also hired some very talented staff comprising security engineering and operations staff, security architects, incident responders, penetration testers, Identity and Access management specialists, and risk assessors.

Most of the security stack now takes advantage of security orchestration and automation capabilities, artificial intelligence enabled by machine learning, and advanced data encryption. The purpose of all these technology upgrades is to defeat threat actors from stealing our sensitive data and intellectual property and other crown jewels within our businesses.

In spite of this sophistication, the technology can still be defeated by the weakest link – the human being. Malicious entities easily exploit users, sending them phishing emails to trick them into surrendering their credentials. They also use other email-based attacks such as spoofing or spamming to entice users into clicking on malicious links. These are also referred to as malware drive-by-download attacks resulting in malware being downloaded and installed on a user's endpoint machine.

CISOs have now hired whole Teams that focus on training and awareness in an effort to train their uses on how to recognize a phishing attack and also to create awareness of common-sense security paradigms both in the professional and personal lives. The most popular theme used in cybersecurity awareness and training programs is "See Something, Say Something".

This chapter builds upon this theme and provides guidance on how to optimize it further.

2 See Something, Say Something

This message has its origins in call to action by DHS to "If you see something, then say something" [1] in response to terrorist attacks on the United States (i.e. the World trade center and the Pentagon on 9/11/01), although this has also been used to highlight the risk of data exfiltration and cyber-attacks perpetrated by insider threat, and makes the point that if an employee notices any odd behavior in the office then they must say something about that to their supervisor, the security team, or to anyone else who would investigate it further or take some appropriate action. (This term is licensed by DHS, but it has allowed the private sector businesses to partner with the DHS in our collective efforts to bring about the needed training and awareness to the public) [2].

I believe this is the beginning of more modern cybersecurity concepts like Zero Trust.

Traditionally, users have inherently trusted other users who may be their peers in the workplace, or even anyone else that may be walking around in an office. They would open doors for other people to get in out of courtesy, help other people badge in into the office if someone forgot their badge, even let them use their user-id to login in case someone's account got locked – and there is nothing wrong with this since it is well established human behavior to trust others and be nice to your friend, your coworker or your neighbor, Right?

Malicious entities and insider threats exploit this somewhat naïve trust in the goodness of human nature. Imposters can masquerade as employees to install malware, conduct espionage or carry out other activities that can bring tremendous financial and reputational risk to a business. These bad actors steal and exfiltrate sensitive data for financial gain or extract revenge for any perceived injustice.

The "See something, say something" theme has been extensively used by cybersecurity, risk management, and law enforcement professionals to combat these threats. Some of the commonly used paradigms are mentioned below:

- If you notice somebody unknown walking around the office, then do ask them for their badge;
- If you notice someone exhibiting odd behavior in the office or trying to access systems or data that they generally don't or shouldn't, then call security;
- If you notice someone is printing out sensitive data and taking it home without prior authorization, then speak up;
- If you notice someone is asking for your credentials as a favor because theirs isn't working, then do not provide and raise the matter with your or their manager immediately;

- If someone asks for your badge since they forgot theirs in their car or home; then do not provide it and also inform security;
- If someone shows sign of intoxication at work; then call security;
- If someone asks for financial loans and promises to return it at the next payday; notify your manager, security and HR;
- If someone is copying data to USB or CD drives, against company policy; speak up about it;
- If someone is receiving expensive gifts from vendors or partners and then subsequently rewards them with contracts; inform the compliance team;
- If you find some new or expensive looking USB drives in the parking lot or on the floor in the office, do not plug them in, but report them to security;
- If you know someone got infected by a virus but isn't reporting it because of embarrassment; talk to them about it and explain to the dangers of not doing so;
- If you notice someone is abusing office equipment by sending or receiving faxes or making phone calls from someone else's phone, especially when they have a phone on their desk; then talk to your manager and security about this;
- If you notice someone is either working from someone else's desktop or is trying to read material off an open screen when the original user has stepped away from their desk; if you witness anything suspicious, then it is your responsibility to say something.

While there are many more examples of causes for concern and response, the bottom line is that this messaging has worked very well. Through training and awareness campaigns (e.g., phishing tests), cyber security teams have dramatically reduced the risk from insider threats, imposters, and other malicious entities.

But do we stop here and declare victory? In my humble opinion there are further optimizations to be extracted and further improvements to be made – as detailed below.

3   See Something, Do Something

Now that we have taken care of the relatively easy and straightforward stuff, let's move to items that are more difficult to deal with but are still very important for us to carry out our cybersecurity mission.

3.1   Making the Case

Let's start with a cybersecurity analogy that will resonate with all cybersecurity technologists. One of the most basic yet effective ways to manage cyber threats is to implement the relatively straightforward and simple security control of monitoring. This control is easy to implement and provides the capability detect and alert against cyber threats like malware or malicious activity perpetrated by insider threats. However, monitoring cannot stop or block the threats; for that to occur, one needs the blocking controls for enforcement action actually to block or kill the malware or stop an insider from exfiltrating sensitive data.

Similarly, the 'see something, say something' saying itself is like a monitoring control. It works well to detect the threats when the people see something suspicious; they report it, but many times an appropriate action to stop may or may not be taken. That's where we have to optimize this to 'See something, do something,' where the person reporting the suspicious activity takes full accountability and responsibility to ensure that a proper determination is made and an appropriate action is taken to remediate the threat in a cybersecurity context.

Some additional ideas are mentioned below.

Removal of Conflict of Interest

To enable and empower cybersecurity professionals to do their jobs, it is advisable that the CISO reporting structure must be such that it removes any organizational conflict of interest.

When the CISO/CSO or other security teams align into the IT organization under the leadership of the CIO, then there may be some conflicts of interest. The security mission is to protect the firm from cyber risk emanating from unpatched systems, deprecated or end-of-life applications or infrastructure, or from new implementations which may not be fully tested for vulnerabilities or securely designed. This may conflict with the CIO's mission to generate revenue and share earnings by outpacing the business functionality of market competition. There are also financial constraints where any funding provided for information security efforts could be construed as funding taken away from the business to invest in revenue-generating opportunities.

According to Gartner "By 2025, 50% of asset-intensive organizations will converge their cyber, physical and supply chain security teams under one chief security officer role that reports directly to the CEO." [4].

The conflict of interest would be resolved if the CISOs reported directly to the CEO as a peer to the CIO. This would enable the CISO and the CIO to make a decision based on risk/reward as equal stake holders, allowing the discussions of speed and agility vs cyber risk mitigation and remediation or risk assumption, when it comes to launching new applications, deferring vulnerability patching and application hardening, or delaying a production release to fix a critical patch or application vulnerability.

Empowerment and Enablement

(a) IT teams often assume risk on behalf of the company when they decide to move forward with software application releases that have (high or medium) vulnerabilities or weaknesses, against security team recommendations. Often in the spirit of teamwork and collaboration, the cybersecurity teams go above and beyond to implement mitigating and compensating controls that would provide suitable (tactical) protections if a given vulnerability were to be exploited by a cyber attacker or malware.

In the spirit of 'See something, do something' *cybersecurity teams should be empowered* to push back against IT teams or the business assumption of undue risk with the deployment of insufficiently vetted applications with known critical, high or medium severity vulnerabilities in production.

Every application or system vulnerability either within an existing production application or a new release destined for a production implementation must be assessed for risk and tracked as a risk finding within a GRC tool. If a given vulnerability cannot be fixed and an application release cannot be held back from going live due to an adverse effect on the business to stay competitive or generate revenue, then the risk/reward analysis must be conducted by the cybersecurity and risk teams and based on the analysis, the business head and the CISO must come to an agreement if the said risk must be accepted or not and if yes then for what duration. Every application or system that is operating in production with known vulnerabilities or weaknesses must have mitigations implemented to prevent the vulnerability from being exploited, with an effort made to remediate the vulnerabilities as soon as possible.

(b) While cybersecurity's sole ownership of the core security systems of firewalls, proxies, domain controllers, authentication and authorizations systems, biometric authenticators and OTP providers, and privileged access management (PAM) systems are generally administered solely by the cyber security team makes them tamper-proof, IT administrative staff's root and administrative access and credentials on most application, database, web servers, other infrastructural components and compute platforms can pose risks to the company's security and its regulatory compliance posture. This manifests itself when proper approvals are not sought from the cyber security team and/or proper change management procedures are not followed. Some examples are discussed below.

1. The unauthorized removal or bypass of security processes and capabilities such as DLP, AV, EDR and dynamic whitelisting by IT systems administrators on endpoints or servers, to perform debugging for unknown application issues.
2. The unauthorized removal or stoppage of security scanning of file shares and other CIFS and NFS file shares citing performance (slowdown) concerns.
3. The unauthorized removal or stoppage of data-at-rest encryption (generally TDE) from databases, citing performance concerns or application issues.

4. The unauthorized downgrade of TLS versions (generally 1.2 to 1.1/1.0) due to application compatibility issues. I would rather fix the application to support the better and more secure version of TLS rather than downgrade the capability because the older application code cannot handle the newer version of TLS.
5. The unauthorized creation or update of IAM roles, or the update of security configurations and ACLs in cloud environments (e.g., AWS or Azure).
6. The unauthorized removal, bypass or disablement of inline security services such as WAF or IPS in production.
7. The unauthorized removal of network segmentation or network zones.
8. The unauthorized removal or bypass of always on (inline) traffic scrubbing services by network admins due to performance (slowdown) concerns.

To enable 'See something, do something' cyber security technologists within the security team must be aware of their role as the information security custodians for the firm so that when they notice or are alerted to IT admins'(unauthorized) activities, they are empowered to request immediate cessation and require that all security capabilities are to be reverted to their former state. In the case of noncompliance, they must also be empowered to declare an incident and report it to the CISO or a delegate from the Cybersecurity Incident Response team. Again "See something, do something"!

No security system, application, process or procedure must be overridden, removed, or shut down without the direct approval of the CISO or a delegate, and the CISO and the security team should not feel pressured to compromise the security posture because of the security team's subordinate status within the IT leadership chain.

The proper way to go about these exercises is to engage the cybersecurity team, explain the problem, get a cybersecurity engineer or analyst engaged, confirm the issue and then collaboratively work together to perform the debugging which may involve the temporary bypass of a security service, feature or capability, and take any other remediation actions using proper change management and control procedures rather than taking unilateral actions that go against the spirit and mission of the cybersecurity policy of a company.

All this can be done while maintaining the purposefully designed separation of roles and responsibilities, and most companies with mature IT and Cyber programs abide by this paradigm!

Separation of Roles and Responsibilities

Ideally, the roles in IT and Security with administrative and privileged access must adhere to a separation of roles and responsibilities. Administrative roles in security and IT should complement one another: IT administrators should not be able to disable or bypass security scanning and monitoring, DLP or data encryption services on application, web, or database servers; security administrators should not have root or administrative privileges for application processes. In other words, IT administrators should never assume the tasks of security administrators, and vice-versa.

Training and Awareness

The role of the CISO and the cybersecurity team is to maintain the confidentiality, integrity, and availability of all systems, to protect the firm from all forms of cyber risk from malware, threat actors or other insider or external malicious entities, and to mitigate reputational risk and risk of fines and enforcement orders by regulatory bodies stemming from lack of compliance with local, state, or federal regulations and policies.

The CISO must instill understanding of the role and mission in the cyber security team to ensure that they can take action when needed. This training and awareness must cover these points:

(a) They must follow the core tenets of the zero-trust paradigm.
(b) They must ensure that the company cybersecurity policy and standards are followed by all vendors, partners, and all internal IT and business staff.
(c) The cybersecurity staff must understand the separation of their roles and responsibilities from the IT staff and must hold the IT staff accountable for any unhygienic or unsecure behavior.
(d) They must know the process to escalate when they observe unsecure behavior by insiders and outsiders alike. The escalation may include the declaration of a security incident.
(e) Every change in a production system – IT, Security or otherwise, must follow proper change management and control processes.
(f) Any unauthorized activity by anyone within the firm must be reported to the security leadership team.

4   The CISO Take

For almost the last two decades the cybersecurity professionals have practiced and preached the security message of 'See Something, Say Something.' To maintain security amid increased threat levels and complex IT and security stacks, cybersecurity professionals must now adopt a more proactive 'See something, do something' posture. This would ensure the full accountability and ownership of efforts to remediate cyber risk across the enterprise.

I have provided a complementary article (chap. 22) that calls for the adoption of a Certification and Accreditation process. This would also further help with the rollout of the 'See Something, Do Something' paradigm for cybersecurity!

5   Definitions

AV – stands for Anti-Virus. It is computer software that has the capability to detect, prevent, block, and remove malware. Most legacy AV uses static (hash-based) signatures to perform the detection [3].

DLP – stands for Data Loss Prevention. It is a technology that prevents the unauthorized access to or exfiltration of company and customer sensitive data [3].

EDR – stands for Endpoint Detection and Response. It is the next generation malware detection system. Rather than relying on the legacy static signature provided by/generated by legacy AV detection products, it has the capability to provide visibility into endpoint user, machine and process behavior, and perform dynamic heuristical analysis, which it then uses to detect and block advanced malware [3].

GRC – stands for governance, risk management, and compliance. It is generally used to refer to the strategy (and the tooling) used to manage an organization's governance, (operational and enterprise) risk management and compliance with local, state and federal regulations, and company security policies and standards.

IPS – stands for Intrusion Prevention System. It is a network security tool that provides monitoring (detection) and protection against network-based attacks and intrusions, including lateral movement [3].

NIST – stands for National Institute of Standards and Technology. It is a non-regulatory US entity with the mission to promote innovation and industrial competitiveness.

PAM – stands for Privileged Access Management. It generally used to refer to a solution that is used to protect, manage, and monitor privileged access and credentials to critical computer systems and applications.

WAF – stands for Web Access Firewall. It is primarily an application firewall that protects an HTTP/S-based (web) application against advanced attacks like cross-site scripting, cross-site forgery, and SQL injection [3].

Zero Trust - is a security architecture and implementation paradigm that reduces enterprise risk by performing secure implementations in compliance with the principal that all assets inside and outside a perimeter firewall are not to be trusted and thus access control for users, devices, systems and services must be provided using least privilege [3].

Disclaimer

The views expressed and commentary provided in this chapter are strictly private and do not represent the opinions or work or the state of implementations or practices within the cyber-security or IT programs of my current or former employer(s).

References

1. DHS. "If You See Something, Say Something®" https://www.dhs.gov/see-something-say-something/about-campaign Accessed March 21, 2021
2. DHS. Partnership and Campaign. https://www.dhs.gov/see-something-say-something/campaign-materials Accessed March 11, Accessed March 21, 2021
3. Badhwar (2021) The CISO's Next Frontier: AI, Post-Quantum Cryptography and Advanced Security Paradigms (Springer)
4. Olyaei S, Thielemann K et al (2021). Predicts 2021: Cybersecurity Program Management and IT Risk Management (Gartner)

My Journey as a Writer

1 Introduction

As I have progressed in my professional journey as a cybersecurity technologist and leader, I have become very passionate about two things in life: first, talking and writing about cybersecurity paradigms as a follow up to years of actually implementing the detective and protective security controls as a cybersecurity and systems engineer; and second, helping others find jobs.

I have talked about my quest to find jobs for the ones in need (especially the veterans that gave their all serving their countries, or the minorities or socially disadvantaged that have struggled to find good employment) in the postlude, but in the context of the topic of CISO Leadership I want to share my very humble journey as a (technical) writer.

2 Early Years

I went to St. Francis School, an all-boys high school in Lucknow, India. This school was established in 1885 during the days of the British 'raj' (rule) and is one of the oldest Catholic schools still operational in India, where the primary medium of teaching is (British and Indian) English. Given that this was India, they also taught us two other languages, Hindi and Sanskrit. As we were growing up in that school system, the teachers, the padres (priests) and the sisters (nuns) never missed an opportunity to remind us that our parents spent good money to send us to this school so that we would not become and talk like a *babu* (a disparaging term used in British India for a clerk). Due to the strict enforcement of the teaching mode in English, all the students in St Francis did have better English speaking and writing skills, and although I was pretty good myself, I felt that I had more proficiency in writing in

Hindi and wrote a couple of poems which were published in the college annual magazine. I believe I lacked the confidence and felt that I couldn't write anything decent in English, but my English teacher (Mr. Robinson) did encourage me and even edited the first piece I ever wrote in English – a Sonnet. It was an original piece but was influenced by Shakespeare and was published in the school's annual magazine (circa 1989-90). I think my days in St Francis really prepared me well to face the (English speaking) world, and I am proud to be a Franciscan.

After I graduated from high school, under-graduate and graduate engineering school, my career as a systems/software engineer in the United States of America (my adopted home) took over and I did not write anything else for the next decade. Well, I did do some writing but it was all (source) code. Although I don't have the accurate stats, I believe I must have written at least two million lines or more of source code in various (computer) programming languages like Cobol, C/C++ and Java during the first fifteen years of my twenty-six-year career as an IT and Security technologist. I also wrote a bunch of technical and design documentation during the same time.

3 Technical Writing

Technical writing, especially about the cybersecurity and IT paradigms, came rather naturally to me because I have always been and still am very hands on with technology.

My first attempt at writing something similar to writing a technology book came when as the chief technologist and head of engineering and architecture for a large defense contractor and systems integrator, I wrote a very detailed 150-page technical engineering management framework (EMF) for the IT and Security services group. Further, my confidence in my ability to do technical writing was boosted during my stints as the head of cybersecurity engineering and operations for some of the largest financial institutions in the world where I also wrote or rewrote almost all their security policies, standards and guidelines. Along the way during the last ten years, I also filed (and received) some security patents, all of which further developed and enhanced my technical writing skills. That led to the writing of my first security book last year, a 435-page manuscript focused on the current and future state cybersecurity technologies, and now this second book focused on the leadership aspect of cybersecurity.

Although I still have a lot to achieve in my cybersecurity career and also plan to write many more security books (e.g., cloud security will be next) – I hope to recall some of the confidence and fundamentals instilled in me by high school English teacher (Mr. Robinson) and write my first non-technical (fiction) book sometimes in the near future as well.

4 The CISO Take

I conclude by highlighting that having good (technical) writing capability is a very important skill to have in cybersecurity leadership roles (like the CISO). From my vantage point, it has helped me tremendously while filing for security patents, writing cybersecurity themed articles for security magazines, writing my blog, making technical presentations to the board of directors, presenting in Gartner peer connect sessions, conducting Lunch-N-Learn sessions, keeping to up speed with changes in security technology and tools, reviewing and writing updated security hardening guidelines, and updating cybersecurity policies and standards in frequent response to the ever-evolving regulatory environment.

Further Reading

RSI Security (2020), WHAT MAKES A GREAT CYBERSECURITY TECHNICAL WRITER? https://blog.rsisecurity.com/what-makes-a-great-cybersecurity-technical-writer/. Accessed on April 18, 2021

Erlin T (2019) Modern Skills for Modern CISOs https://www.tripwire.com/state-of-security/security-awareness/5-modern-skills-modern-cisos/. Accessed on April 18, 2021

Death D (2019) Ten Must Have CISO Skills https://www.hellersearch.com/blog/ten-must-have-ciso-skills. Accessed on April 18, 2021

Goodchild (2019) It Takes Restraint: A Seasoned CISO's Sage Advice for New CISOs https://www.darkreading.com/edge/theedge/it-takes-restraint-a-seasoned-cisos-sage-advice-for-new-cisos-/b/d-id/1335716. Accessed on April 18, 2021

Tripwire Guest Author (2021) The Security Wisdom of the All-Knowing CISO https://www.tripwire.com/state-of-security/security-data-protection/the-security-wisdom-of-the-all-knowing-ciso/. Accessed on April 18, 2021

Defensive Measures in the Wake of the SolarWinds Fallout

1 Introduction

As most of you may be aware, nation state-sponsored hackers breached software provider SolarWinds to inject a type of malware called "Sunburst" into the SolarWinds' Orion software platform. Sunburst is a trojanized malware signed with valid digital certs, and contains a back door used to communicate with command and control (CnC) servers on the dark web [1].

Apart from some very big names (e.g., FireEye and Microsoft) that disclosed their exposure in December (2020) and January (2021), many more entities including many cyber-security vendors have now also disclosed that they were also targeted and breached by the SolarWinds supply chain attack.

While most of these (software) vendors claim that they have contained the attack and have taken mitigating actions, the fallout continues.

2 Generic Defensive Measures

Implementing a defense-in-depth scheme using the various best practices defined below is going to be critical in defeating SolarWinds and other sophisticated malware and better managing third-party cyber risk.

R. Badhwar, *The CISO's Transformation*, https://doi.org/10.1007/978-3-030-81412-0_9

2.1   Enable Improved DNS Alerting Using a DNS Sinkhole

Deploying a Domain Name Service (DNS) Sinkhole, a technique that helps with the identification and blocking of DNS requests from malware infected hosts on a private network, can prove very effective in detecting suspicious DNS traffic using malicious techniques like DNS tunneling. It enables the redirection of malicious internet-bound traffic by entering a fake entry into a DNS server to change the traffic flow of a malicious URL. The sinkhole allows corporate cybersecurity teams to control any Command and Control (CnC) bound traffic and other malicious traffic across a private network. In addition to sinkholing malicious traffic, this technique can also be used to deploy kill switches against malware. Additional modern ML techniques such as Shannon Entropy on real-time DNS traffic, can also be used to alert against such attacks.

2.2   Deploy Malware Kill Switch

The kill switch kills or terminates a ransomware process, sometimes working in tandem with a sinkhole to do so. It is generally a file which crashes the parent process when the ransomware attempts to enumerate or encrypt it. This technique can be proactively deployed to work against a generic class of ransomware. Kill switch files are generally pushed to high-risk endpoints or servers by security teams as defensive measures.

The kill switch can also be backdoor into the malware with a command interface that the attacker may have left open to kill the process if/when needed, that can now be used by cyber defense teams.

2.3   Perform Monitoring and Alerting Enhancements

To perform cross-functional analysis and create alerts to detect SolarWinds-type attacks, use supervised or unsupervised deep learning machine learning (ML) algorithms to enable real-time full traffic packet capture from network SPAN or TAP ports. These cross-functional alerts within a security incident and event management (SIEM) system with automated orchestrated reactive response will be the only effective way of stopping these attacks.

2.4 Detect Golden SAML Attacks

The Golden SAML cyber-attack forges SAML responses and bypasses IdP authentication to access federated services via SSO. This attack builds on the traditional Kerberos attacks such as pass the hash (PTH) or golden or silver ticket (attacks) on Active Directory (AD) where the attacker gains privileged access (e.g., domain admin) on an AD domain controller. To distinguish golden SAML attacks from legitimate SAML authentication events, correlate SP login events with corresponding authentication events within the Identity Provider (IdP) and AD domain controllers (DC), and identify the SP logins using SAML SSO which do not have corresponding events in the DC. To identify golden SAML attacks, detect any of the following: an export of an IdP certificate (to extract the private key), the addition of new custom SAML attributes or modification of existing attributes, and the addition of a new trusted (yet malicious) IdP.

Enabling the capability to detect the reuse of user authentication tokens by different IP addresses, auditing Kerberos traffic, or detecting a sudden spike in (kerb) service ticket requests can also be used as detection triggers.

2.5 Reconsider the Usage of DOH

While the usage of DNS over HTTPS (DOH) is beneficial to maintain the confidentiality of DNS requests, it can also be used by malware to hide malicious DNS tunneling requests. Thus, if the capability does not exist to perform a TLS inspection of DNS traffic, then I recommend that the use of DNS over HTTPS be disabled for corporate environments where visibility into DNS traffic is required to enforce corporate information security standards and gain visibility into malicious DNS requests from corporate networks.

Apart from this, some additional enhancements may be to block all newly registered internet domains for 48 hours, proxy all DNS requests, and block port 53 for outbound DNS requests from internal endpoints and servers. (Internal Endpoints and servers should be configured to use internal namespace servers, not those hosted on the internet.)

2.6 Better Manage Third-Party Risk

The capability to gain visibility into third-party risk by implementing a threat Intel platform, access to third party breach information and follow general security hygiene protocols can prove beneficial in determining the risk of third-party network and security breaches. Also, critical to attack prevention is capability to assess the integrity of the software build and delivery process used by vendors to protect themselves from injection of malware, and dependency and namespace confusion attacks.

3   SolarWinds Specific Actions

While the generic actions detailed in the previous section will help provide the needed protections from all forms of third-party risk, this section will provide some additional tactical steps that can be used immediately against the SolarWinds specific threat.

- Deploy threat hunting capability on all network endpoints.
- Implement robust threat monitoring in development environments.
- Reset all credentials used either in using or managing the Orion platform.
- Develop a process to verify the integrity of all inhouse software being built.
- Subject the Orion environment (including any new feature/functionality and security patches) to sandboxing, penetration testing and forensics examination.
- Re-sign all the software associated with the Orion platform with new digital certificates once they've been sanitized and verified to be clean.

4   The CISO Take

The CISOs have to learn from the SolarWinds breach and implement detective and blocking level controls to protect their enterprises from the whole genre of third-party attacks. Apart from all the security controls they must also use threat intelligence from private and public sources to gain knowledge about any indicators of compromise that can be loaded into endpoint and network security modules and also available for event co-relation within the SIEM.

The CISOs must also impress upon the software vendors, partners and integrators to enable the capability to verify the integrity of the software that is built and delivered by them so that malicious backdoors and malware cannot be injected into any software or firmware delivered either by a third party or built in-house.

5   Definitions

CnC – stands for command and control (server). It is generally a cloud-hosted server/system using DGA-generated domains used by threat actors to control and manage infected and breached endpoints and servers (generally resident) on private networks [2].

DNS – stands for Domain Name System. It is a global naming system which enables the mapping and the subsequent syncing of a website or other internet/intranet-hosted resource name, to an IP address [2].

DNS Sinkhole – stands for Domain Name Service Sinkhole. It is a technique that helps with the identification of malware infected hosts on a private network. It enables the redirection of malicious internet-bound traffic by entering a fake entry into a DNS server to change the traffic flow of a malicious URL. The sink-hole allows to control any CnC bound traffic and other malicious traffic across a private network. These can also be used to deploy kill switches against mal-ware [2].

Pass-the-hash (PTH) – it is a common AD exploit where an attacker impersonates a user by stealing the cryptographic hash of their password and uses it to authenticate as the user [2].

SAML – stands for secure access manipulation language. It is a standardized mechanism that enables an identity provider (IdP) to assert an identity by passing its authentication and authorization credentials to a service provider (SP) to help enable paradigms like SSO. [2]

SIEM – stands for Security Incident and Event Management (System). This started out as log repositories but now have the capability to provide real-time cross-platform correlated analysis of security events and alerts from all the security systems and applications within an enterprise environment [2].

Disclaimer

The views expressed and commentary provided in this chapter are strictly private and do not represent the opinions of or implementation at my current or former employer(s). Any advice provided here must not be construed as legal advice. If you choose to follow any advice provided in this book, then you must do so at your own risk.

References

1. FireEye (2020) Highly Evasive Attacker Leverages SolarWinds Supply Chain to Compromise Multiple Global Victims with SUNBURST Backdoor. Available via FireEye Blogs: Threat Research. https://www.fireeye.com/blog/threat-research/2020/12/evasive-attacker-leverages-solarwinds-supply-chain-compromises-with-sunburst-backdoor.html Accessed 15 April 2021
2. Badhwar (2021) The CISO's Next Frontier: AI, Post-Quantum Cryptography and Advanced Security Paradigms (Springer)

Further Reading

Krebs B (2020) Malicious Domain in SolarWinds Hack Turned into 'Killswitch.' Available via Krebsonsecurity. https://krebsonsecurity.com/2020/12/malicious-domain-in-solarwinds-hack-turned-into-killswitch/ Accessed 15 April 2021

Rashid FY (2020) Stopping Solarwinds backdoor with a killswitch. Available via Decipher. https://duo.com/decipher/stopping-solarwinds-backdoor-with-a-killswitch Accessed 15 April 2021

Reiner S (2020) Golden SAML Revisited: The Solorigate Connection. Available via Cyberark Threat Research Blog. https://www.cyberark.com/resources/threat-research-blog/golden-saml-revisited-the-solorigate-connection Accessed 15 April 2021

Cimpanu C (2020) Microsoft and industry partners seize key domain used in SolarWinds hack. Available via ZDNet. https://www.zdnet.com/article/microsoft-and-industry-partners-seize-key-domain-used-in-solarwinds-hack/ Accessed 15 April 2021

FireEye (2021) Sunburst Information https://www.fireeye.com/current-threats/sunburst-malware.html Accessed 15 April 2021

Part II
Cybersecurity Team Building

Cyber Exceptionalism

1 Genesis

I first wrote this little piece for an internal company blog on Veterans Day in 2019, as I sat in an airplane while waiting for it to take off. It had been the usual busy day as a cyber-security professional, starting with a full day of meetings in the office, capped off with a two-hour cab ride from Hartford to Boston and a long wait at the airport to take an international business trip. I couldn't let that day pass without sharing a message regarding Veterans Day and expressing some additional thoughts on how we could apply the spirit of military service to cyber security. I try to blog frequently on an internal company blog to evangelize cyber security to all company employees but I have customized this message for external consumption.

2 Introduction

On this Veterans Day, I salute all our veterans, the band of brothers and sisters that were injured while fighting for our country, and the ones who gave their lives so that others could live freely. These were and are exceptional human beings. I want to draw from this exceptionalism that they have displayed on the conventional battleground and extend it to introduce the concept of cyber exceptionalism (something that took root in my mind when I did some work as a chief technologist for a defense contractor in the field of security services).

R. Badhwar, *The CISO's Transformation*,
https://doi.org/10.1007/978-3-030-81412-0_10

3   What is Cyber Exceptionalism?

It is that belief that makes $1 + 1 = 11$, that together we can deliver much more than we can deliver as individuals; it is our common mission that binds us together and makes us cyber security folk as one; it is that sense of exceptionalism that provides us the self-belief that irrespective of the challenge, our backgrounds, our countries of origin, the languages we speak, the religions we practice, or if we argue in favor of Linux over Windows (or vice-versa), or 'C' over 'Java' (or vice-versa), or otherwise - when we make this bond of shared commitment, we become one and exceptional. Veterans have taken part in conventional warfare and now cyber security professionals engage in cyber-warfare. We have been entrusted with the responsibility of protecting our industry, our businesses, our employees, our customers and clients, our partners, and our peer companies from cyber-attacks launched by malicious entities, spammers, hacktivists, threat actors and some sophisticated advanced persistent threats (APT).

4   Who Can Be Cyber Exceptional?

Teams of cyber professionals enter what I call a state of cyber exceptionalism when all team members share the common mission of maintaining the confidentiality, integrity, and availability of systems, services and sensitive data, defending their organization against various cyber-adversaries and attackers. They are exceptional when it is no longer a 9-5 job, when it becomes a mission that is only a close second to family. They are exceptional when the security of the company's systems becomes the source of collective team honor and pride. They are exceptional when a security professional would go the extra mile for a peer, no matter what the need may be. They are exceptional when your coworkers are not just office mates but a band of brothers and sisters. Cyber teams are exceptional when they work together selflessly to create and share best practices for preventative and protective security controls, anonymized and de-personalized indicators of compromise (IOCs) and other threat intelligence gathered from public and/or private sources with others. They collaborate with peer companies and businesses to form a shared defense and provide information to entities that are not or cannot take part with shared threat information sharing platforms like FS-ISAC.

5   How Can One Become Cyber-Exceptional?

There is no one single recipe to achieve this, but there are a few underlying principles: believe in the cause of cyber security, be passionate, and put in the hard work required to become a subject matter expert, to be the best in that one role that you may play or the task that you may perform. You may be a cyber-security engineer for network, endpoint, or web security; a cyberoperations expert for the tools in a company's security stack; a malware analyst; a SOC analyst; an incident responder; a risk analyst; a security architect; a security compliance analyst; or a data scientist. Think about soldiers who go to war, getting paid a fraction of the salary that they may make commercially, while putting their lives on the line, all because they believe in the core mission of protecting one's country, and the way of life and freedom of its citizens. Similarly, if we performed the various cyber-security engineering, operations, and incident response functions with the same zeal and passion individually, and then pooled our resources and skills with our internal team members and maybe even external partners to work collectively, we could create an exceptional cyber-workforce with our cyber-core code being, "Protect, Educate, Innovate" with the ability, confidence, and self-belief to take on any cyber-adversary.

Also, CISOs must band together to create non-profit cybersecurity training institutes or provide similar services for actual returning veterans and other under-served (diverse) individuals who could be a value add to the cyber workforce, but who do not have the training or the means. I would also recommend that the government provide post-service veteran job training funds for CISO-created organizations that may do this type of work.

Lastly, I want to take this opportunity to honor our fallen cyber security professionals who may have provided expertise in the areas of cryptography and cryptology in their day jobs but served their tours of (military) duty abroad in the signals intelligence (SIGINT) function. They were truly selfless and exceptional human beings.

6   My Cyber Journey

As part of this chapter, it is only apt that I also share my own IT and Cyber journey. As I was coming up the food chain as an IT and Security professional, I overcame some hurdles and stereotypes. I generally don't talk or write about these experiences but am doing so now with the hope that this may help others that may find themselves with similar challenges.

The first hurdle was to overcome the stigma and limitations of H1-B! I grew up in India, where I also completed high school and my undergraduate degree in electrical and electronics engineering, but only worked in that country for a couple of months. Essentially, all my professional career has been in the United States of America. I started my software and security engineering career while working on an H1-B (work) visa in the US, where I also attained a graduate degree in information systems from George Washington University. While I was on H1-B, due to visa program restrictions, I could not get promoted or pursue other internal or external job and career advancement opportunities, even though I had both the qualifications and the skills. I was doing some really interesting work and had acquired subject matter expertise in many key IT and Info security areas – leading to a lot of frustration. It took a decade to attain permanent residency and US citizenship, but I eventually went on to work as a Security leader for some of the largest corporations in the world, accumulating many Security and IT certifications along the way. Once I became a naturalized US citizen, I was able to serve my adopted country in my own way when I worked for the federal defense contracting establishment, obtaining a Top-Secret Security clearance. After years of striving for professional advancement, trying to be flexible in the face of real obstacles, my defense contracting work gave me perspective on my challenges. If many of our veterans and soldiers wounded in battle have overcome challenges associated with PTSD or other severe and debilitating injuries to do amazing work later in their careers, then the limitations and stigma of the H1-B should not and cannot bring me down or limit my ability to be a technologist and leader in area about which I am passionate.

As a head of cyber security for multiple firms, I had the opportunity to lead some returning veterans hired as cyber security analysts. While I knew they had the required security clearances, I thought, with my expertise, I could teach them various cyber security engineering skill sets. Instead, I learned a lot more from them about leadership, teamwork, dedication and perseverance. As the supposed lead security expert of that team, I have to admit that they taught me more than I could teach them.

Another hurdle I faced was the stereotype that Indian Americans make good programmers and developers, but can't be managers or leaders, especially in the cyber security space. I was told by a few mid-senior level leaders in some of the firms I worked 10–15 years ago that it would be best if I stuck to engineering and architecture type roles. Sometimes you lose faith in yourself when you're repeatedly told that you can't do something, but I also found some great mentors in my career who coached me into pursuing my leadership goals. I was able to get some pretty cool gigs, serving as cyber security Director and VP for some of the largest firms in the world. Always believe in yourself and your abilities; it is good to have aspirations and goals, but you've got to follow them up with grit and hard work. One of my mentors, Kevin DePeugh, the former CISO of AIG, told me, "You've gotta work twice as long and hard as the other guy, if you want to be the best in the industry." I still practice and preach that work ethic. We live in a vibrant and diverse country and community, but there will always be some stereotypes that need to be broken and changed. Who better to do that than you? Lead the way in making things happen. The opportunities and potential for success are limitless if you have the right can-do attitude and the will to succeed.

7   The CISO Take

I personally strive for this cyber exceptionalism and want to bring this message and attitude to the rest of the cyber-security eco-system of our peers and partners. I call on your support for this cause and for our cyber-core motto of "Protect, Educate, Innovate".

I also recommend we foster better partnerships with other internal associates within a firm, modeled after the close working relationships between IT and Risk professionals and cyber-security personnel – collaborating with our internal and external peers and getting the security message out is key to the success of this mission.

8 Definitions

APT – stands for Advanced Persistent Threat. It is used to describe a campaign of attacks by persistent sophisticated threat actors whose intent is to gain long-term residence or presence on the network of the target. The list of malicious activities includes but is not limited to stealing intellectual property or company sensitive data, sabotaging key network segments or systems, installing and operating backdoors to communicate with CnC servers, and conducting complete site take-overs. These attacks are complex, targeted, well-resourced and funded, and are generally conducted by nation states or other criminal organizations.

AIG – stands for American International group. It is one of the largest and most iconic insurance companies in the world.

CISO – stands for Chief information Security Officer. It is the custodian and executive officer of the first line of defense for the cyber security and information technology security and risk program for a given organization. [1]

CnC – stands for command and control (server). Generally, a cloud-hosted server/system often working in tandem with the usage of DGA-generated domains, the CnC is used by threat actors to control and manage infected and breached endpoints, and servers (generally resident) on private networks. [1]

IOC - stands for indicator of compromise. It is either a unique signature, log entry, or an event that indicates that a network or system breach has occurred. These can be used as forensic evidence, either individually or in combination with other IOCs. [1]

SIGINT – stands for signals intelligence. It is the gathering of intelligence generally conducted by intercepting radio and electronic signals (and waves). It is part of the overall intelligence community (IC) workstream.

SOC – stands for Security Operations Center. The SOC represents the combined capabilities provided by security professionals (generally resident in a secured physical space), processes and technologies with a mission to provide 24×7 security, network and application monitoring services for a given enterprise.

References

1. Badhwar (2021) The CISO's Next Frontier: AI, Post-Quantum Cryptography and Advanced Security Paradigms (Springer)

Further Reading

NSA (2020). What is SIGINT? https://www.nsa.gov/what-we-do/signals-intelligence/ Accessed March 10, 2021

Skovlund M (2019) THE LEGEND OF CHIEF SHANNON KENT https://coffeeordie.com/shannon-kent/. Accessed March 10, 2021

Smeets M and Shires J (2017) PART 4: "Cyber Exceptionalism" https://www.newamerica.org/cybersecurity-initiative/c2b/c2b-log/cyber-exceptionalism/ Accessed March 10, 2021

Legacy (1971-2019) Kevin DePeugh https://www.legacy.com/obituaries/wiltonbulletin/obituary.aspx?n=kevin-depeugh&pid=191864915

Special Needs, Disability, and Cybersecurity: Often, a Great Fit

1 Making the Case

Some time back, before the onset of the pandemic, I was sitting at an airport waiting to catch a flight when I noticed a 10–12-year-old child with a school backpack on his back, running around the terminal mumbling and randomly stopping and saying things that I somewhat understood (since he was speaking one of the six languages I understand) but that logically did not make a whole lot of sense to me. He also had some deformed teeth, wore a food-stained shirt, seemed disoriented, and would not make eye contact with anyone. Although I do not have any expertise in this area, he seemed to be a child with special needs. Perhaps he was on the autism spectrum.

The child's mother was sitting couple of rows away with two other much younger kids. Most of the seats were taken and eventually, when the child wanted to sit down, there were few unoccupied seats. When he found one and sat down, the person sitting next to him was so disgusted that he looked around with an angry expression on his face, as if he wanted to find the child's mother to tell her to manage her son. Although the child did not say anything to the person, touch him, or take any action to make him uncomfortable, the person was visibly irritated by mere proximity, as if the child had the plague.

Eventually he curtly told the child to stay away from him, at which point I stood up and offered to exchange seats with the person and sat down next to him. A few minutes later, the child took out an iPad from his backpack and started playing with it. I tried to make some conversation with him, and asked him his name using the language he was speaking earlier, and then asked him in English. He gave me a blank stare. Later I noticed that the child was looking at some mathematical pictorial puzzles on his iPad, and so I again asked him if he liked math, at which point, he nodded his head, still without making any eye contact. I then asked him some basic addition and multiplication questions and the child spoke to me and got them all right. Then I upped the difficulty level a bit, and again, he got them all right. I am

© The Author(s), under exclusive license to Springer Nature
Switzerland AG 2021
R. Badhwar, *The CISO's Transformation*,
https://doi.org/10.1007/978-3-030-81412-0_11

not a math whiz myself and wanted to test him further, but then I would have had to take out my iPhone to calculate bigger numbers to quiz him. Eventually his mother came for him.

Based on my initial impression of him, I would not have thought he would be able to answer some of the two- and three-digit multiplication questions I asked him. I certainly would not have expected it from most 10–12-year-olds, but he pleasantly surprised and humbled me with his advanced mathematical acuity.

While this is not a traditional cyber topic, I think the message here is that people with special needs or other disabilities, whether they were born with them or acquired later in life, are to be treated with respect and kindness. What we call 'normal' behavior is something that we have defined based on our own convenience and norms but human consciousness has various forms, many of which we do not yet understand. None of us are perfect. I know I want to throw a 95-mph fastball or an 88-mph curve ball like Max Scherzer or acquire Roger Federer's forehand skills or Serena's serve or play chess like Viswanathan Anand, but I can't. I just don't have the capability to achieve those skill levels. My limitations do not make me an inferior person. I do a lot of things in my personal and professional life that these folks can't do; similarly, people with special needs and disabilities have skills and capabilities too that need to be developed, harnessed, and appreciated. They may not always fit societal norms and expectations, but they might excel in some areas where people with typical abilities do not. We need to give them an opportunity to share those abilities with us to give a meaning and purpose to their lives and enhance our own lives. This is why we need to embrace rather than shun those who may be different.

Cyber security is an area that is way ahead of other forms of employment when it comes to providing an equal opportunity to people with disabilities. Defense contractors, especially cyber security and IT teams within those firms, have made a serious and concerted effort to hire Afghanistan and Iraq War veterans. Many of these returning veterans had suffered serious physical or mental trauma, and afterward, simply needed a chance to do meaningful work. These veterans were a natural fit for cyber security work, especially in the federal space, as most of them already had the security clearances, and, after some basic training and experience, they became capable cyber security intelligence analysts, system administrators, systems operators, project managers, or security engineers. Cyber security teams within the defense contracting world and within the financial sector have put their money where their mouth is, hiring many of these returning veterans. Corporate America may not get everything right, but this is one area where they have stepped up to the plate and deserve many kudos!

2   The CISO Take

Cyber security teams have much to gain by hiring people with special needs and disabilities, who may possess a range of talents which can meet the needs of employers. People with disabilities often have unique skills; in particular, people with autism sometimes have highly developed mathematical skills in pattern matching and detection and in other areas of computation that many average people cannot decipher. Research on the utilization of training data sets in moving from supervised to semi-supervised and then to unsupervised machine learning and artificial intelligence algorithms helps us understand how humans learn. Once these algorithms are trained, then they can perform some amazing analysis (e.g., monitoring and response) at machine speed – there is no magic here and this is not science fiction; this is simply taking an algorithm and training it with data to give it artificially intelligent performance capabilities. Similarly, we have humans who may already possess the raw capability to analyze data and perform computing operations. With specialized training, such individuals can make significant contributions to security teams and other fields.

Note that although I have focused on STEM-related pattern recognition as a strength of people on the spectrum, it is important to recognize this as a mere subset of all individuals who identify as being on the spectrum. Given that the employment rate for people with autism and other disabilities is abysmally low, corporations could identify alternative methods for recruiting individuals with a range of previously unseen, underutilized abilities and talents.

Yes, we may have to invest as a society and solicit help from corporate America in supporting education and training and additional recruiting, funding ABA (applied behavioral analysis) therapy for autistic children or adults, finding opportunities for people with Down's syndrome, ensuring the provision of special needs supports at engineering schools for students with autism spectrum disorder (ASD), or retraining those who have returned from the battlefield. We also have to make a serious and significant effort to recognize their potential and understand how they may operate at different levels consciousness with unique ways of perceiving the world. This will prove mutually beneficial both to employers, increasing their bottom line, and to the direct recipients of such training and education.

3 Definitions

Autism Spectrum Disorder (ASD) – Autism is a bio-neurological developmental disability that generally appears before the age of 3 [2].
Applied Behavior Analysis (ABA) – Is a therapy provided to people on the autism spectrum [1].
Asperger's Syndrome – Has been associated with advanced language skills and intellectual ability, including but not limited to pattern recognition. Since 2013, it has become part of the umbrella diagnosis of Autism Spectrum Disorder (ASD) [4].
Down Syndrome – is a condition where a person has an extra chromosome [3].
STEM – stands for Science, technology, engineering, and mathematics. It is a is a broad term used to refer and group these academic disciplines as a curriculum choice within schools in the English-speaking world.

References

1. Autism Speaks. Applied Behavioral Analysis (ABA). https://www.autismspeaks.org/applied-behavior-analysis-aba-0 Accessed 5 Dec 2020
2. National Autism Association. About Autism. https://nationalautismassociation.org/resources/autism-fact-sheet/ Accessed 5 Dec 2020
3. National Center for Birth Defects and Developmental Disabilities, Centers for Disease Control and Prevention (2020) Facts about Down Syndrome. https://www.cdc.gov/ncbddd/birthdefects/downsyndrome.html Accessed 5 Dec 2020
4. Autism Speaks. What is Asperger Syndrome? https://www.autismspeaks.org/types-autism-what-asperger-syndrome Accessed 5 Dec 2020

Further Reading

What Is Autism? https://www.autismspeaks.org/what-autism Accessed 5 Dec 2020

National Center on Birth Defects and Developmental Disabilities (NCBDDD), Centers for Disease Control and Prevention (2020) What is Autism Spectrum Disorder? https://www.cdc.gov/ncbddd/autism/facts.html Accessed 5 Dec 2020

Deloitte. Children with special needs learn about cyber security through gaming. https://www2.deloitte.com/nwe/impact-report-2019/articles/hacking-for-special-needs-students.html. Accessed 5 Dec, 2020.

NICCS. Veterans: Launch a New Cybersecurity Career https://niccs.cisa.gov/training/veterans Accessed March 11, 2021

CyberVirginia, Cyber Veterans Initiative https://www.cybervets.virginia.gov/ Accessed March 11, 2021

BAE Systems Inc. Military & Veterans https://jobs.baesystems.com/global/en/militaryveterans Accessed March 11, 2021

Why employers should hire veterans https://www.baesystems.com/en-us/our-company/about-us/bae-systems-inc/community-investment/remember-honor-support/why-hire-veterans-infographic Accessed March 11, 2021

Bias-Free Lexicon

1 Introduction

The language of cybersecurity and information technology is the professional language of the professional workplace, focused on subjects relating to business technologies and systems and cyber threats and attacks. Professional ethics warrant that workplace language is free from extraneous influences, with the expectation that the language and the cognitive frameworks on which our workplace discourses are based are as polished as our shoes and as tidy as our dry-cleaned office attire. However, a cursory glance at some common terms used to describe technology suggests that our language may fall short of our expectations of professionalism.

This chapter describes the biases of our workplace language, reasons people resist linguistic reforms, our counterarguments to such resistance, and the ways in which workplace language can either promote professionalism and excellence, or prove detrimental to teamwork, even derailing the effectiveness of the cybersecurity team.

Why is linguistic bias a cybersecurity problem? Don't cybersecurity professionals have enough problems to solve? Linguistic bias is an enterprise-wide problem. We've all known about this for a long time but have not taken steps towards reform. The security team led by their CISOs are known for resolving difficult issues, for enforcing security policies against pushback and resistance from their IT peers, and are the ones that can take on this new challenge and lead the away to correct this behavior.

2   Shoring Up Professionalism in the Workplace

Many common computer science (CS) engineering-related terminologies have been used for decades. They have been part of our engineering curriculums in college and then become frequently used standard terms throughout professional IT and Security careers. The IT and cybersecurity terms in this somewhat random sample list demonstrate the nature of the problem: abort, master, slave, child, brute force, execute, hung process, turn off/on, whitelist, white hat, blacklist, and black hat.

Our assumption that the language of the professional sphere is nothing less than professional and unbiased belies the prima facie meanings of these terms. If, reader, you were not aware that these terms were applied to technology, and you were asked to write a story using these words, just imagine the kind of story you would write. It would have slavery, race, sex, and death as its themes! While reading literature with these themes may help us critically explore the implications of our cultural history, using such language in the workplace threatens to make us unwitting proponents or even subjects of such themes, undermining the roles for which we are hired as professionals.

3   What's the Impediment to Linguistic Reform?

If most of us possess such a strong commitment to our profession, then how and why do we bring biased, potentially offensive elements of language into the workplace?

There are two tendencies in human language which address this question. First, regardless of context, all human communication entails the frequent use of metaphor. Metaphors are not mere poetic devices; instead, they are derived from the socio-cultural frameworks shaping the way experiences are organized conceptually [1], even though we may not be fully or even partially aware of their influence over our conceptual thinking [2]. When using metaphor, a speaker applies a supposedly analogous concept in one domain to something else in another domain, connecting disparate, and not necessarily relevant, aspects of our experience.

Therein lies our problem with our workplace language - descriptions of issues specific to the professional workplace are over-reliant on metaphors derived from socio-cultural frameworks, which themselves are often based on categorical folk theories [3]. Our samples are metaphors based on folk theories about power imbalances and notions of good and evil based on comingled Western themes of slavery, race, sex and death. Indeed, behind the face of every professional is also an ordinary human being, whose views of the world may be rooted in specific cultural prejudices, either consciously or unconsciously maintained, that would not hold up to the kind of scrutiny we should expect in the workplace.

Reliance on folk theory to describe technical processes is untrustworthy on many levels: it is inaccurate, it can potentially cause group division rather than promote unity, and it can be harmful to the mission of cybersecurity.

With regards to the lexical inaccuracy of our workplace language, there is nothing, for example, inherently or perceptibly white or black about hacking. No graphically real and brutal executions or hangings occur. A brute force attack does not involve actual physical violence, contrary to what "brute" implies. No actual children, masters, or slaves are involved in these processes. Although this is an obvious point to make about metaphors, it is important to acknowledge that these terms are, in a sense, detached from the reality of the wires, chips, and processes they reference.

The application of this array of metaphors to a body of technological systems should immediately erase any notion that technologists consistently adhere to objectivist technological or scientific rationality free from social or cultural influences. The use of folk categories, especially deeply problematic ones, suggests a lack of self-scrutiny, undermining efforts to behave with professionalism.

It is worth noting the basic values of cybersecurity, viewed from the lens of the (various types of tangible and intangible) assets-as-property ownership framework: The purpose of information technology and security is to build systems that maintain and protect ownership of assets. To the technologist, threats to systems and assets are bad; protections are good. Malicious hackers are, in fact, bad. Systems which can exert control are powerful; systems subject to control are weaker. When a process or system fails, it may seem as though life itself has ended.

When giving this description of basic values, I have pared down the egregiously offensive content. Although I have mostly avoided the taboo metaphorical references to slavery and sex, I have still described assets in metaphorical terms – whether assets are financial, digital, electronic, or a market brand, they are all categorized as types of property, to be owned with attached rights or traded in exchange for stock or capital. For better or worse, our society is organized around property ownership. As long as metaphors referring to things owned do not cause offense (as they did, say, in Maoist China or revolutionary France), then then the notion of good and evil pinned to the property metaphor is likely acceptable in a corporate setting. Choosing acceptable language is a matter of negotiating meaning on a foundation of universal respect for every employee and current and potential client [4].

The Fig. 1 below provides a sample of some terms that could be improved with alternative bias-free terms. As obvious from the comments, not only are these terms bias-free but are also more accurate.

With Bias	Bias-Free	Comments
Abort	Stop, cancel, end	Cancel a process or procedure.
Black hat	Malicious entity or criminal or hacker	Used for external penetration tests. Also used for malicious actors.
Blacklist	Denylist	In firewall rules, proxy configuration and DLP control lists
Child (folder) Child (process)	Subfolder Sub process	In directories. In Linux/windows processes.
Master	Primary or Parent	In message queues, processes and servers etc.
Process is hung	Process not responding	In OS or application processes.
Slave	Secondary or child	In message queues, processes and servers etc.
Turn (on) Turn (off)	Power (on) Power (off)	For computers and systems.
White Hat	Ethical hacker	Use for penetration testing
Whitelist	Allowlist	In firewall rules, proxy configuration and DLP control lists
White Paper	Technical paper	Technical documentation and papers
Execute	Run	For Linux/Windows processes and jobs.

Fig. 1 Biased Lexicon and Bias-free Alternatives

The second tendency in human language is that when a particular metaphor is used frequently enough, then it actually begins to refer to the thing referred to in the second domain: the name for a non-STEM-based folk theory concept becomes the term for the technical concept. People then use it without considering the original meaning. When someone uses terms such as "white paper" or "blacklist," they may not be giving any thought to the question of race or misconstrued cultural associations of color with good and evil. People may even resist efforts to reform the language of the workplace, offering points of resistance based on notions such as:

(a) **Convenience** – It's the way I was taught and thus its easier this way.
(b) **Tradition** – It's what we've always called it, and so why change now?
(c) **Cost** – It is cost-prohibitive to make these changes.
(d) **Training** – I don't want to re-train all my users with the newer terminology and lexicon. It's just language; how do words affect my work?

3.1 Response to Impediments

A CISO response to some of the impediments listed above is provided below:

Convenience and Tradition – Arguments for "convenience" and "tradition" are oblique forms of resistance to change. Given that cyber security involves the frequent learning of new technologies and getting certifications to develop advanced technical skills and knowledge, it seems strange to argue for the importance of tradition. Arguments for tradition fall squarely within the bailiwick of the luddite – what on earth delineates tradition in Security or IT? A laptop instead of an iPad? A desktop instead of a laptop? IBM RACF controls instead of Microsoft's Active Directory controls? A castle moat over a badging system? Cyber security technologists would be ineffective if they were luddites refusing to understand advanced technological concepts such as artificial intelligence or machine learning; why would they argue for tradition unless they are viewing their social world from outdated and perhaps privileged socio-cultural frames? Our framing of the social world needs to be updated just as our technological world does.

The argument that it is inconvenient to make these lexical reforms is actually an insistence on maintaining non-technological folk theories, with demonstrable potential to perpetuate inequalities and promote workplace dysfunction. It is, unfortunately, no coincidence that this list of metaphors is largely constructed around gender and race and violence, in a time when Human Resource Departments still must often deal with issues related to inequitable treatment of employees stemming from gender and race discrimination. The repeated use of offensive terms is, if anything, wholly *inconvenient* for companies.

Cost – Yes, there may be a short-term cost increase from the time/effort put into the institute this change, but the (long term) costs of not doing anything are much higher. The cybersecurity and IT teams of the present cannot fall into the tactical legacy IT cost save (or cost avoidance) trap of the past.

The steepest cost of maintaining an offensive, rather than welcoming and inclusive, language in the workplace is the inability to retain current talent, or, if a company develops a bad workplace culture reputation, to hire potential talent.

In fact, if you cannot develop a diverse team, your team may not be as smart or as effective and efficient as it could be [5]. Additionally, more diverse teams actually provide better security, especially in areas such as Artificial Intelligence. Human linguistic and cognitive biases can lower the quality and robustness of AI inputs, resulting in biased AI [6].

Making a concerted effort to improve the *environment* of the team may improve the *work* of the team and prove to be *cost effective*. It may even prove crucial to making a company *more profitable* based on better AI development.

Training – Newer lexicon may seem to be a minor change to some people, but every mindful change in language and rapport to be more aware and respectful of differences in backgrounds will align employees' socio-cultural frames with higher standards of workplace inclusivity and professionalism. Such change can be a springboard for other changes, with one type of change hopefully amplifying into additional methods of building an equitable and inclusive workplace culture.

Training in language, then, is actually an exercise in improving both the security team's cohesiveness and its work product, which in the case of cybersecurity, is the security of the company.

4   Corrective Behaviors

There are several techniques and corrective behaviors we can follow to identify and correct of these biases in our lexicon.

(a) **Training and Communication** – Talking about change should not be uncomfortable. Having the appropriate training and awareness program can be instrumental in making improvements and help in getting the message across to the workforce.

(b) **Recognition of potential harm** – Making an effort to raise awareness about the potential harm that this kind of lexicon may inflict on certain individuals is very important. Not everyone's social or cultural reality is structured by the same set of metaphors, [7], and as the examples demonstrate, metaphors may reference things which have no place in the workplace and have the potential to cause discomfort.

(c) **The power of Inclusion** – Reshaping a team's lexicon will also send the right message about the team's seriousness about their intent to be inclusive of members with diverse backgrounds and cultures.

(d) **Building a style guide** – Correction is needed at a systemic level. An approach that can easily be implemented is to create a style guide that can be referenced by all parties concerned about the proper verbiage that can be used going forward for all new product, project and program specifications guides and documentation.

(e) **Adoption and Operationalization** – After publishing the style guide and training the team responsible for its evangelization, then it can be rolled out to the entire company. Steps can also be takes to get broader partner-level adherence, evangelization and acceptance.

5   The Next Step

I give kudos to companies like Microsoft [8], Google, and Apple, among many others that have led the way by publishing their bias-free style guides to update existing documentation and by writing new product/process documentation and guidelines.

We can only be successful in our respective missions for equality, diversity, and security when we remove all impediments to progress. While we have made some progress in promoting acceptance of diversity of thought, race, orientation, culture and belief, we also have to remain open to the fact that we need to examine and re-examine our implicit biases regularly, whether in the ways that we speak and write, or in our IT and Security product features, documentation, and guides.

CISOs are leading this transformation within their respective organizations and I call on your support to make this happen. Leading an ongoing group effort to develop and use more inclusive language will foster cohesiveness rather than division.

6   The CISO Take

Who but the security professionals! The cyber security personnel continue to deliver on their mission to protect their enterprises and firms from various threat vectors both internal and external, domestic and state sponsored. To us it's not a 9–5 job, we are the marines of the IT world – we take on challenges and solve difficult problems and do whatever it takes and however long it takes to deliver on our mission. We go the extra mile, all the time. To us it's just not about protecting the integrity and confidentiality of the data and systems under our purview, but we also take pride in doing the right thing protecting the integrity and ethics of our profession by doing what we can to protect our society, the commonwealth, the infrastructure; and by acting honorably, honestly, justly, responsibly, and legally [9].

Although workplace culture is usually a concern for human resources departments, cybersecurity teams may also be uniquely positioned to promote a conscious effort towards bias-free language. Cybersecurity teams are used to pushback in implementing their security policies and technologies; they are well equipped to deal with cultural resistance to social change. Social change is to the social fabric, what security is to the functioning of the company.

The Cybersecurity teams can be a BRIDGE for getting others throughout the company to accept a bias-free lexicon in all IT domains and business areas. As goes the leader, so goes the rest of the crew.

This is definitely not an easy task. It first begins with recognizing that this is a valid problem. When I look back at some of the terminologies I used in my last book (e.g., firewall and access control whitelists and blacklists) [10], I realized that instead of being a proponent of this change, I myself learned and used language embedded with unconscious biases. We can only defend against all threat vectors when we have an inclusive workforce that is all-in into our cyber mission without any distractions whatsoever.

Given the potential for the outsized impacts of biased linguistic inputs on the quality of AI and on the composition of our cybersecurity teams, the commitment to professional excellence in cybersecurity demands that we regularly pay attention to our language.

7   Definitions

DLP – stands for Data Loss Prevention. It is a technology that prevents the unauthorized access to or exfiltration of company and customer sensitive data.

ISC2 – Is an international, nonprofit membership association for information security leaders. It offers many certifications including but not limited to CISSP.

CISSP – Certified Information Systems Security Professional. Is a security certification granted by ISC2 who meet the minimum criterion and pass a comprehensive exam.[1]

Style Guide – is a set of standards for writing product specifications or documentation. It helps to provide a uniform and consistent style across the written (technical and non-technical) specifications, guidelines documentation and marketing material.

References

1. Robertson, S (2020) Foundations in Sociology 1: Module 12: Collective Resistance and Social Change. https://openpress.usask.ca/soc112/chapter/collective-resistance-and-social-change Accessed 22 Feb 2021
2. Lakoff G and Johnson M (1980) Metaphors We Live By, U Chicago Press, Chicago and London, p 3.
3. Lakoff G (1987) Women, Fire, and Dangerous Things: What Categories Reveal about the Mind, U Chicago Press, Chicago and London, p 118.
4. Lakoff G and Johnson M (1980) Metaphors We Live By, U Chicago Press, Chicago and London, p. 231.
5. Rock D and Grant H (2016) Why Diverse Teams Are Smarter https://hbr.org/2016/11/why-diverse-teams-are-smarter Accessed 18 Apr 2021
6. Henry J (2020) Biased AI Is Another Sign We Need to Solve the Cybersecurity Diversity Problem https://securityintelligence.com/articles/biased-ai-is-another-sign-we-need-to-solve-the-cybersecurity-diversity-problem/. Accessed 18 April 2021
7. Lakoff G (1987) Women, Fire, and Dangerous Things: What Categories Reveal about the Mind, U Chicago Press, Chicago and London, p 415.
8. Microsoft (2020). Bias-free communication. https://docs.microsoft.com/en-us/style-guide/bias-free-communication . Accessed 13 Feb 2021
9. (ISC)² (2020) Code of Ethics Canons. https://www.isc2.org/Ethics Accessed 13 Feb 2021
10. Badhwar R (2021) The CISO's Next Frontier – AI, Post-Quantum Cryptography and Advanced Security Paradigms, Springer Nature Switzerland AG.

---

[1] The Author holds an active CISSP certification.

Further Reading

Bowers D, et al (2020) Is Your Communication Bias-Free and Inclusive? https://www.marketing-partners.com/conversations2/is-your-communication-bias-free-and-inclusive   Accessed   22 Feb 2021

Cohn, C (1987) "Sex and Death in the Rational World of Defense Intellectuals." Signs, vol. 12, no. 4, 1987, pp. 687–718. JSTOR, www.jstor.org/stable/3174209 Accessed 23 Apr 2021

Klein J (2020) Being Inclusive across Microsoft 365. https://regarding365.com/words-are-important-d819ccd33f57 Accessed on 20 Feb 2021

Lakoff G and Johnson M (1980) Metaphors We Live By, U Chicago Press, Chicago and London

Lakoff G (1987) Women, Fire, and Dangerous Things: What Categories Reveal about the Mind, U Chicago Press, Chicago and London

The Grass Is Not Always Greener on the Other Side

1 Introduction

Recently on a security leadership ideation session, I was asked about the issue of attrition in the cybersecurity community. For those that may not know, there is a significant global shortage of cybersecurity personnel, leading to the constant churn of associates from one company to another in the cyber world, primarily driven by the allure of better compensation or job satisfaction.

While it is easy for a cyber security professional to rely on the tactic of frequently changing jobs to chase slight salary hikes or to get away from current workplace problems, this chapter recommends more deliberate forms of devising a personal career strategy, whether through mentoring, certifications, skills development, or accepting the current role as it is.

2 Happiness and Job Satisfaction

Although jumping ship every other year for a 5–10% salary increase does not look good on your resume and is not a good career development strategy, I am supportive of moves driven by a desire to improve your family's economic circumstances. However, I humbly request that before you make that move, you also think about the cybersecurity team relying on your part in a collective effort to deliver on our mission to protect our firm, our employees, customers, and partners from threat actors.

Also, from a career perspective, my message to Cybersecurity personnel is that if the move is seeking greater happiness, more job satisfaction, or better projects somewhere else, then remember that the grass is not always greener on the other side. Trust me, I can say this based on my personal experiences and observations over my last 25+ years in Cybersecurity and IT.

R. Badhwar, *The CISO's Transformation*, https://doi.org/10.1007/978-3-030-81412-0_13

If a cybersecurity professional is leaving an employer because of the lack of support or understanding from their managers, then I would recommend that they bring the issue up with their Manager, HR or even their CISO. I know that most CISOs are all about the team and generally would do their best to either remove toxic managers or act as a catalyst for change to help improve employee/manager relationships. Our mission to protect our enterprises and eco-system is way too important and cannot be held hostage by toxic managers or leaders.

3   Don't Burn Your Bridges

If one were to take another job for any of the reasons mentioned before then I recommend that you leave on good terms with your current security team and its leadership, and not burn any bridges. Give the recommended 2–3 weeks of notice, do not bad mouth or say disparaging things about your soon-to-be former security team and/or leadership.

After you have left the employment of your current company, do not divulge any confidential or sensitive information that you may have been privy to during your employ with them, either deliberately or in passing. This information may include but is not limited to weaknesses, vulnerabilities, or incidents in your former employer's IT or application environments.

The security community is a small world. We keep in touch with each other and these days many of the good security positions are hired through referrals and references.

If there were to come a time when the better paid position that you left becomes unavailable or if you were to become a victim of cost cuts or workforce reductions, then having good working relationships with a former team or their leadership could still reopen that door for you if you were to decide to walk through it, but all this is predicated on those relationships remaining intact.

4   Get a Mentor

I have personally observed people in the cybersecurity industry make frequent tactical jumps from one employer to another chasing 5% salary hikes or for other reasons.

If cybersecurity is your long-term career of choice, then you must design, develop, and follow your own career roadmap. Having a good mentor, generally a CISO or another Senior Security leader, is extremely useful in creating and charting this career roadmap. A mentor can give you feedback on your strong and weak points, help you focus on areas for improvement, point out the companies you should keep on your radar, provide guidance on certifications important to your path, help you identify the right time to change jobs, and dissuade you from job decisions solely driven by short-term financial gain.

Being mentored by two former CISOs really helped me plan my career. Even though life or career events can sometimes be beyond our control, in spite of meticulous planning, the advice I got from my mentors has been instrumental to my advancement.

I have also realized (and so should you) that this is a journey. The learning never stops. We are all trying to get better at what we do while ensuring that we take care of our families, but we should be mindful of the consequences of tactical moves of questionable relevance to our overall strategic plan for our career. Such moves can really prove detrimental to one's professional growth in the long run.

5   Other Implications

Many cyber security professionals come from backgrounds in the military, the intelligence community or the military industrial complex. Many have security clearances that would need to be refiled if they were to move jobs. While the security clearance should not act as an impediment to career growth, the lengthy time period required for refiling or transferring a security clearance from one employer to another should be factored into a decision to change jobs. Speaking from a personal experience, when I moved my job from a defense contractor to the private sector, I lost my security clearance. If my current job or future job were to require one, then it would take me at least 2 years to get another clearance.

6   The CISO Take

I do want to state for the record that the idea of happiness and job satisfaction in the next job is a mirage. We need to strive for happiness and job satisfaction in our current circumstances. Unless we give up on the idea that job satisfaction and cool work is somewhere else, it will never be where we are today!

CISOs are responsible for reducing employee attrition in their organizations. To maintain cybersecurity employee compensation levels at the industry standard, CISOs must ensure robust funding for their program. The cyber risk from anything more than a 5–7% employee churn is too high for the overall security and hygiene of an enterprise.

Although there are always exceptions, I recommend junior to mid-level cybersecurity personnel to stay at a given employer for at least 4 or 5 years. This is required to gain the breadth of experience one needs to be a successful cyber security technologist and professional. Follow your career path and passion for cyber security. Trust me, the money will automatically follow you rather than the other way around.

Further Reading

Oltsik J (2020) The cybersecurity skills shortage is getting worse. https://www.csoonline.com/article/3571734/the-cybersecurity-skills-shortage-is-getting-worse.html Accessed 18 Feb 2021

Sayegh E (2020). As the End Of 2020 Approaches, The Cybersecurity Talent Drought Gets Worse. https://www.forbes.com/sites/emilsayegh/2020/09/22/as-the-end-of-2020-approaches-the-cybersecurity-talent-drought-gets-worse . Accessed 18 Feb 2021

Belli G (2019) ARE YOU JOB HOPPING TOO MUCH? https://www.payscale.com/career-news/2019/04/are-you-job-hopping-too-much. Accessed 18 Feb 2021

Lee M (2019) Stop Looking for the Purple Squirrel. https://www.isaca.org/resources/isaca-journal/issues/2019/volume-2/stop-looking-for-the-purple-squirrel-whats-wrong-with-todays-cybersecurity-hiring-practices. Accessed 18 Feb 2021.

Stuart G (2019) When Job Hopping Isn't Worth It. https://news.clearancejobs.com/2019/08/02/when-job-hopping-isnt-worth-it/, Accessed 18 Feb 2021

Badhwar (2021) The CISO's Next Frontier: AI, Post-Quantum Cryptography and Advanced Security Paradigms (Springer)

Let Not Any Outage Go to Waste

1 Introduction

Everyone hates outages – that includes the security team. When these unplanned outages occur, the cybersecurity teams are generally the first teams called upon to assist and they play a key role in the debugging, remediation or mitigation of the issues – collaborating with their IT and Application peers. But let's be real, IT system outages in production are a reality in this day and age, not only because of super complex information technology applications and systems but also because of the high rate of change owing to the adoption of agile software development and deployment methodologies which can (sometimes) lead to code that is not thoroughly tested into production if proper due diligence is not performed. This commentary is not about outages and whether the adoption of agile methodologies have led to the increase or decrease of outages as compared to say the legacy waterfall model etc. – rather it is about how can we make the best use of outages when they do indeed occur.

2 Making the Case

Generally when a production outage occurs we have ALL the (otherwise hard to get) right people on the conference bridge opened in an effort to remediate the issue – the application developers (to debug the application), the database administrators (to look at the DB), the storage guys (to check if there are storage issues), the network admins (to look for networking, DNS, routing type issues), the business analysts, the (QA) testers, and the security guys (to look at the firewalls and other tools in the security stack). I think this is a great opportunity to identify and document any application or system flaws or issues and get *real-time feedback* from all the subject matter experts to best to solve the issue at hand both tactically and strategically, maybe have a discussion about architectural deficiencies, talk about the scope for any application performance optimizations, network routing improvements, better and/or faster data replication, DB query optimizations or the need for an index on a key table that is becoming a bottleneck, load balancing and app level security improvements etc. etc. *This would be something like a real-time RCA (root cause analysis) + improvement ideation* session. Also, if opportunity presents itself, these outages are also good opportunities to test the disaster recovery *readiness* and business continuity *management* aspects of the application or system in question.

Please take note that all the ideas that are identified, need to be brought back to a lower-level environment and then properly implemented and tested in lower environments before they make their way back up-to production.

This is just a security guy trying to think out of the box to make best use of the opportunities given to us to bring about application/system/network/security optimizations and/or improvements.

3   Change Management

With change in the infrastructure, application and security stack, the change management team has to change as well. Gone are the days where the Change Advisory Board (CAB) would meet once a week using a waterfall approach and agree upon the changes to be made, line up all the developers that would be deploying (or pushing) the change, the security folks that would making the appropriate DNS or firewall changes, the QA team doing the testing, and the business representatives performing application checkout all in a tight window over a given weekend.

The rapid rate of change due to the cloudification of the infrastructure stack, the CI/CD pipeline that is delivering incremental bi-weekly or month code and application releases, requiring very frequent prod and even more frequent pre-prod/dev/qa changes, requires an agile change management process that can accommodate these paradigms.

And we should not be abusing the eCAB (emergency CAB) process either to push these changes, since the eCAB is only meant for emergency security or application break-fix changes.

The new paradigm calls for daily (or twice a week) change windows where code may be able to be pushed to lower-level environments for testing and verification, and maybe also to production.

In the cybersecurity world, one paradigm that is now prevalent is to allow additions of security configuration (FW rules, Proxy adds, DNS adds, etc.) on a daily basis but then do the updates (including removals) over the formal (larger) change windows during the weekend.

Performing business checkout on a daily basis after application or security changes in production is not very feasible and thus this is only possible if the changes and especially the verification cycles are automated. It is easier to run a script or have a bot (attended or unattended as the case may be) perform the verification rather than have humans login in during the wee hours of the night every day to perform the needed verification to confirm that a change did not break functionality or create a security hole in production. The cybersecurity teams have capabilities like dynamic application security testing (DAST) that can be used to perform quasi penetration tests in an automated manner every time a change is pushed to an internet facing application to ensure that a security hole has not been created with a specific deployment or configuration change.

One other item that comes to light from the various outages is the fact that at least half the time the changes work just fine in pre-production environments but fail in prod – WHY? The reason is obvious, most of the times the lower-level environments are not replicas of production. At least one pre-prod environment must be an exact replica of production, so if anything is tested there and it works then it must not break in production. Investing in (more) lower-level environment and keeping them in alignment and sync with production is extremely important and can reduce production code implementation issues by up to 50%.

4 Operational Ownership

Another way to reduce outages in production is to re-examine operational ownership of the infrastructure stack. In spite of getting all the groups together in a CAB session, there are many times when the right hand is not talking to the left hand and changes either go bad and have to rolled back due to lack of coordination or cause SEV1 (P1) issue.

Given the high rate of change, the exponential increase in cyber threats and attacks, the cloudification of our infrastructure stack with the introduction of hybrid cloud (IaaS, PaaS) working in conjunction with on-premise hosted infrastructure and systems, it is my recommendation that ALL networking and compute infrastructure be operationally owned by the CISO team. The security team has an active hand today in almost all these infrastructural components – nothing can be pushed to prod without the security team either making a security configurational change (e.g., FW), conducting a penetration test, scanning an application for vulnerabilities, subject it to sandboxing for behavior analysis to account for third party risks, assign a machine identity (using an internal CA), enable authentication and/or authorization (including certificate management), DNS or routing changes among various other processes and thus a lot gets lost in translation changing hands between the application, infrastructure and security teams during these production deployments. The production outages can be further reduced by changing operational ownership to the security team especially for cloud heavy environments with higher than normal and more complex than normal rate of change.

5   The CISO Take

Let not any production outage to go waste. A lot of improvement and optimizations can either be done right away during outage resolution or identified for further improvements for a subsequent release.

Also improving and optimizing our change management processes and making them ready for the cloudified ecosystems and re thinking operational ownership of cloud hosted systems are other areas that can increase stability and productivity for our applications and systems.

6   Definitions

CA – stands for certificate authority. Is an entity that issues digital certificates [1].

CAB – stands for Change Advisory Board. It is a group of IT, Security, Business owners and other key decision makers, whose mission is to evaluate proposed changes to an IT environment.

CI/CD – stands for continuous integration and continuous delivery. It is a modern application development paradigm of delivering code (changes) more frequently and more reliably.

DAST – stands for dynamic application security testing. It allows the developers or automated processes (e.g., scripts) to find vulnerabilities and weaknesses within a running (web) application by using fault injection techniques [1].

DNS – stands for Domain Name System. It is a global naming system which enables the mapping and the subsequent syncing of a website or other internet/intranet-hosted resource name, to an IP address.

References

1. Badhwar (2021) The CISO's Next Frontier: AI, Post-Quantum Cryptography and Advanced Security Paradigms (Springer)

Further Reading

Ritchey D (2020). The Changing Role of the CISO. https://www.securitymagazine.com/articles/91653-the-changing-role-of-the-ciso. Accessed on Feb 21, 2021

Mathenge J (2020). Change Management in the Cloud https://www.bmc.com/blogs/cloud-change-management/. Accessed on Feb 21, 2021

Google (2020). Managing Change in the Cloud. https://services.google.com/fh/files/misc/managing_change_in_the_cloud.pdf

Froehlich A (2017). IT Outages, Who's Really at Fault? https://www.informationweek.com/strategic-cio/executive-insights-and-innovation/it-outages-whos-really-at-fault/a/d-id/1328869

Lightstep (2020). Best Practices for Root Cause Analysis. https://lightstep.com/rca-best-practices/. Accessed 21 Feb, 2021.

If You Can't Hire Them, Then Develop Them

1 Introduction

One of the problems facing CISOs is the acute shortage of qualified cybersecurity personnel. The shortage can be severe enough to challenge the capacity of a cybersecurity team to protect its enterprise. While CISOs expend personal effort and use their clout to secure the funding to hire the qualified and skilled security personnel for their program, once they find the right resources, they must contend with the issue of retention. This chapter details the problem statement and provides ways on how to develop and retain cybersecurity talent.

2 Develop the Talent

Due to widely diverse application development languages, operating systems, application and web servers, databases, directories and various other tool suites running either on endpoint machines or resident on systems or servers hosted in on-premises and disparate public or hybrid cloud environments, the skillsets required to operate the various cybersecurity tools that secure these ecosystems are equally diverse and complex. The security engineers who work on these tools are in high demand. Even when you do find them and hire them, there is a good chance that you may not be able to retain them, especially those who are skilled in the newest technologies and have the niche specializations skills.

There are three ways of dealing with this problem. First, management could pay its way out of this predicament by offering the best compensation for that industry segment. Secondly, it could farm out the work to contractors. However, this is definitely not cheap and when a contractor leaves or when they are no longer affordable, all the knowledge walks out the front door. Finally, management could take the risk

© The Author(s), under exclusive license to Springer Nature Switzerland AG 2021
R. Badhwar, *The CISO's Transformation*,
https://doi.org/10.1007/978-3-030-81412-0_15

of delayed projects due to key subject matter experts leaving for better pay then struggling to find qualified replacements.

A different approach that I recommend you take is to develop these subject matter experts and key resources in house. Hire entry-level college computer science or mathematics majors and train them as security engineers. You can also pre-identify these college graduates by running an internship program and then invite the interns you think would be good fit for your program once they graduate, by offering them entry-level positions. The training should be conducted by a core group of senior engineers and architects who are compensated very well and have other retention packages that would keep them from being lured away by your competitors. I also recommend that you continue following this approach to have a good pipeline of young and smart engineers, so that the engineers your team developed into smart security technologists leave only after 4 or 5 years (and yes, they will leave, but not before giving you a good number of years of stability). You will then have a continuous supply of new security professionals to take their place.

The other reason to develop fresh graduates into security engineers is to meet the need to have people skilled in newer complex security tools or in the plethora of cloud native tools that keep showing up on the horizon every 6 months. It is otherwise next to impossible to find and hire these qualified security engineers externally.

Some of the additional points to consider while building the capability to develop security talent are mentioned below.

2.1 Technology Aptitude

Candidates that have a focus, active interest or inclination towards computer software or hardware or technology in general, are generally a good fit for cybersecurity. The capability to self-learn various technology subjects like programming or scripting languages can be a great building block for a cybersecurity professional.

To assess technology aptitude or focus in prospective candidates, there are several modern techniques. Gamification Assessment relies on interactive and immersive use cases to gauge technology interest and provide real-time feedback on technology aptitude. Advanced behavior analysis and mining of data from prospective candidates consist of looking at their school and/or college work, whitepapers or articles, postings on technology-oriented social media platforms such as LinkedIn, Twitter, Reddit, Quora, Stackoverflow, and Stackexchange.

2.2 Flexibility

In this hybrid state of IT located both in the cloud and on the premises, one of the core tenants of dealing with the plethora of a cyber program's various security tools is to strive for skillset diversity and maintain the flexibility to learn new skills. Once such candidates are identified for these traits, you can then hire people who already know or are ready to learn a wide variety of tools spanning the multiple security domains of the endpoint, network, data, perimeter, and cloud.

A CISO must lay out this vision and requirement of this flexibility and adaptability to the security hiring managers who would be interviewing fresh college graduates and other entry-level candidates.

2.3   Business Domain Awareness

One thing that is equally important to programming skills or flexibility is having the capability to understand the business. A cybersecurity engineer will never be fully aware of all the threats until they understand the business domain. This trait must be judged in the potential entry-level candidates by looking at their ability to

(a) **Conduct Research or interviews** – Any past history of writing business or technical papers that require research and writing or conducting interviews with project stakeholders.
(b) **Business Degree or Certifications** – A college major or minor in business or business certifications like Salesforce, supply chain professional, business analysis professional or actuarial experience.
(c) **Business Internship** – Internships within business groups or any other exposure to business domains.

2.4   Mission Focus

To be successful in the cybersecurity field, one needs to realize that it is not a traditional nine-to-five job. The job is driven by our mission to protect the confidentiality integrity and availability of our systems and services, and sometimes we end up working long weeknight and weekend hours. If prospective candidates don't have the drive and passion required to realize and deliver on our mission, then they would not make good candidates to be developed as future cyber technologists and incident responders.

2.5   Systems Thinking

The prospective candidates should be systems thinkers and have the capability to understand how systems or parts thereof interact with each other and operate as a whole.

Systems thinkers are silo-brakers, think about inter-connected systems (processes and procedures) that may have both linear or non-linear relationships.

2.6   Problem Solving

The ability to solve complex problems is another key skill that is very important in cybersecurity. This also includes the capability to think outside the box or established norms, processes, or perspectives.

Systems thinkers (who also make great problem solvers) further breakdown problem solving into the following processes –

- Problem Identification
- Problem Definition
- Information Gathering
- Solution(s) Development
- Solution(s) Evaluation
- Solution Selection
- Continued Solution monitoring and optimization

2.7   Collaboration

Cybersecurity is a team sport. Our motto is 'United we stand or divided we shall fall.' You can only succeed in this field with total commitment to teamwork and collaboration between the various security domains and capabilities.

The prospective candidates must be willing to collaborate with all members of the cybersecurity team to do whatever is required to fight against the threat actors and vectors.

Given the round-the-clock nature of the work, ensuring that cybersecurity teams can build in work-life balance could be important in retaining employees. Collaboration also entails pulling in double shifts to cover for our co-workers who need time off to take care of family or personal matters.

2.8   Expand the Net

Generally, cybersecurity or IT teams try to bring in interns or hire engineering graduates with formal degrees in computer science and information systems. While this has worked very well for us, in my long career in cybersecurity, I have come across some great cybersecurity professionals who majored in music or accounting.

I believe the timing is ripe for the cybersecurity teams to expand the net and looks for potential candidates coming from diverse educational backgrounds and training. The technology can be taught but the acumen and analytical aptitude are sometimes inherent and can be discovered in the right candidates. The diversity of training, thought, culture, and experience only make us better and stronger.

2.9 Trust

One last trait I'd like to talk about is trust. We cybersecurity professionals trust our internal co-workers and external peers to work together in our mission to protect our enterprises from advanced threat vectors. If we can't place our trust in each other, then we cannot be successful in doing our jobs.

Managers should gauge the extent to which members of the team engage with one another and weed out lone wolves who seem to have inherent issues trusting their coworkers. Sometimes, the obstacle to team engagement is an individual employee or the manager. Sometimes, the obstacle to teamwork is the overall atmosphere of the workplace. Managers should strive to foster environments free from biases based on gender, ethnicity, race, or class background. This can involve consideration of anything defining the workplace experience, from workplace language, employee interactions, the nature of after-hours teambuilding events, to workplace scheduling arrangements.

3 Retention

Whether it is the new talent that we developed or hired, or existing mid-level or senior talent, one of the most important tasks to successfully run and maintain a stable and effective cybersecurity program is to retain these individuals.

Although the overall goal is retention, the strategies vary by the three employee categories below –.

3.1 Entry-Level

For new recruits, either fresh college graduates or other talent being developed (as described earlier in the chapter),

(a) Foster an environment that transcends gender, ethnic or racial differences, and is conducive to teamwork.
(b) Ensure effective periodic mentorship by and job shadowing of senior team members and management.

(c) Provide frequent constructive feedback.
(d) Invest in suitable training resources to help them succeed in their assignments.
(e) Make them active contributors by entrusting them with challenging projects.
(f) Foster a spirit of cyber exceptionalism (see Chapter "Cyber Exceptionalism" for more details).

3.2   Mid-Level

(a) Emphasize career growth by helping to identify paths to cyber security team lead and manager opportunities.
(b) Emphasize on the work-hard, play-hard approach, and support their pursuit of other growth opportunities such as advanced education, training, and cybersecurity certifications.
(c) Encourage them to publish research and whitepapers to internal and external audiences, and to apply for patents.
(d) Implement project-based (cash) incentives for successful completion of key initiatives delivered on time and within budget.
(e) Implement an annual short-term incentive (generally cash) as part of a rewards and retention program.
(f) Set expectations for behaviors striving toward Cyber Exceptionalism.

3.3   Senior and Executive Level

(a) Implement and enroll into executive leadership development programs.
(b) Encourage executive education programs (Executive MBA).
(c) Encourage them to be present at cybersecurity forums and security conferences such as Gartner and RSAC.
(d) In addition to annual short-term incentives (generally cash), provide longer-term incentives (generally stock) as part of a retention and rewards program.
(e) Provide exposure to the company's executive leadership, such as the CISO, CIO, CRO and CEO, by either inviting the CXOs to security staff meetings or by inviting the security leaders to present in quarterly executive or risk committee meetings.

4   The CISO Take

The only way we can overcome the cybersecurity worker shortage is with strategic development of a talent pipeline of people with needed cybersecurity skillsets. CISOs must get the funding to hire and retain experienced professionals who in turn will train fresh college graduates and promote behaviors that are conducive to teamwork.

The CISOs must also lead from the front and give their team members a sense of their mission – to protect, innovate and educate!

Definitions

BBA   stands for bachelor of business administration
CIO   stands for chief information officer
CISO   stands for chief information security officer
CRO   stands for chief risk officer
CXO   C Level executives
MBA   stands for master of business administration

Further Reading

Immersive Labs (2020) Cyber security talent is expensive – so why not develop your own? https://www.immersivelabs.com/resources/blog/cyber-security-talent-is-expensive-so-why-not-develop-your-own/. Accessed 20 Feb 2021

Emsi (2020) A Skills-Based Strategy to Solve the Cybersecurity Talent Shortage. https://www.economicmodeling.com/cybersecurity/. Accessed 20 Feb 2021

Tech HQ (2020) Make or buy? 5 tips for fostering cybersecurity talent. https://techhq.com/2020/12/make-or-buy-5-tips-for-fostering-cybersecurity-talent/. Accessed 20 Feb 2021

Morgan S (2019) Cybersecurity Talent Crunch to Create 3.5 Million Unfilled Jobs Globally By 2021. https://cybersecurityventures.com/jobs/. Accessed 20 Feb 2021

Arnold, Ross & Wade, Jon (2015) A Definition of Systems Thinking: A Systems Approach. Procedia Computer Science. 44. 669–678. https://doi.org/10.1016/j.procs.2015.03.050.

RSA Security Conference. https://en.wikipedia.org/wiki/RSA_Conference

Gartner Security and Risk Management summit https://www.gartner.com/en/conferences/apac/security-risk-management-australia/agenda

Badhwar (2021) The CISO's Next Frontier: AI, Post-Quantum Cryptography and Advanced Security Paradigms (Springer)

Should You Accept Counteroffers?

1 Introduction

Should one accept counteroffers or not? I have recently read many articles on LinkedIn and other forms of inter-webs, and have also heard various IT and security leaders give strong opinions on this topic.

The general consensus and the supposed rule of thumb cited is "never accept a counteroffer" – Right?

The argument given is that if you really hate your job so much and if the current firm has not done enough to recognize your talent, then why would the firm suddenly promote your interests upon your acceptance of a counteroffer – Right?

How will acceptance of a counteroffer dramatically change a situation to cure all perceived issues– Right?

Also, conventional wisdom suggests a counteroffer is a short-term tactical win for the current manager, who will either let you go when convenient for the company or not follow up on any additional promises made regarding your advancement – Right?

Numbers don't lie: It seems like the statistics are all in the favor of the so-called rule of thumb – Right?

I am not going to advocate for or against any rule. All I want to do is to share my perspective and advice on this matter from both employee and employer points of view.

I also want to discuss how general employment prospects for cyber security professionals may slightly skew conventional notions about counteroffers, and briefly share my personal experiences as a manager on this matter.

© The Author(s), under exclusive license to Springer Nature Switzerland AG 2021
R. Badhwar, *The CISO's Transformation*,
https://doi.org/10.1007/978-3-030-81412-0_16

2   General Advice and Comments

While many of these points may be true and the stats may all be alluding to one answer, never blindly follow this "never accept a counteroffer" rule of thumb.

The decision to accept (and offer) a counteroffer is situational, to be made in the context of the firm you work for and your relationship with the team and the management. Trust should factor into your decision here. Trust has to be earned based on what you may have observed or your past experiences with the manager or the employee, as the case may be. Always consider all the facts in play before making a decision.

I can assert here that not all leaders are alike, and I do not have any residual hard feelings against an individual who may have (or not) accepted a counteroffer. I think it's a learning experience for both the employee and the manager: for the manager, to learn about issues that may exist within the organization; and for the employee, to ascertain the extent to which they and their work are valued in the organization they are trying to leave.

3   Advice to Employees

If you really feel that you're a fish out of water and want to find another job, then you should follow your heart.

On the other hand, if you like the firm, the people, and the culture, but you also believe the current team or its management is holding you back from fulfilling your potential, then you should seriously consider a counteroffer with a role and responsibility that will help you do better. Ideally, it should never come to your resignation, but if you have resigned, then you should at least consider a counteroffer.

If you feel you can make a difference for yourself and for your peers given the right opportunity, and a counteroffer may help you achieve that, then you should seriously consider a counteroffer.

Trust is everything. If you trust the management is sincere about providing you the right growth opportunities, then you should consider the counteroffer.

Do not use a counteroffer as a tool to get a pay hike or promotion. If you feel you are underpaid or underemployed, then you should have an honest conversation with your manager. If you feel that the manager may not be too sympathetic to your cause, then you should ask for a skip-level meeting with the manager's manager, and definitely talk to the HR manager as well. Employee satisfaction is very important to most of the firms these days, and there as various ways to express your desire for a reconsideration of your job or your pay. I can say from personal experience that in all the cases where I have been approached by an employee with a similar matter, the outcome has always been a positive one (directly) for the employee and (indirectly) for the firm.

My final advice on this matter is - Instead of chasing money, acquire new skills, develop your talent, and show your passion. The money will always follow - trust me!

4 Advice to Managers

Never offer a counteroffer as a tactical short-term stop-gap measure. If the employee is genuinely not a good fit in the team for whatsoever reason and has resigned, then do not try to retain the employee while secretly planning to replace them later – you're doing the team, the employee, and the firm a disservice.

Always think about the interests of the employee and the team first. If retaining the employee in a similar or different role helps the team, then you should follow up with a counteroffer.

If you have given a counteroffer to an employee, then you must be sincere in following up with any promises of advancing the career prospects, or re-evaluating the job-scale or the pay-scale of the employee in question.

Never let pride get in the way of recognizing and correcting any problems within the team or the company, leading to a given employee trying to leave. Do not get upset if an employee wants to hold a skip level meeting with your manager, it is their right and it is your responsibility to make sure that they are given that opportunity to pursue this right for open dialog and feedback.

Counteroffer or not, always take any feedback provided by a departing employee as constructive criticism.

5 The Cybersecurity Skew

As we all know, the high demand for cyber security skillsets has been a boon to cyber sec professionals, who often receive more lucrative, career-advancing external offers at a faster rate than our non-cyber peers. For corporate leaders tasked with developing strong security programs within budgetary constraints, this poses a challenge – However, I have had good success in getting counteroffers accepted by cyber sec engineers with an intent to leave for greener financial pastures.

Good cyber sec professionals are always hard to find and replace when they leave. Given the nature of our work, cyber security professionals are more receptive to the concept of teamwork and our collective mission of protecting the data and systems of our customers and employees, than their non-security peers.

Given the global shortage of cybersecurity talent and evolving work from home scenarios, CISOs have to deal with the increasing risk of having their precious cybersecurity talent lured away by vying competitors or other entities with deeper pockets. Also, given that the cybersecurity is a specialization over IT skills, there is growing trend of internal IT teams trying to hire cybersecurity talent as Senior IT engineers (with higher compensation) further exacerbating the cybersecurity shortfall.

To retain employees with cybersecurity skillsets, leadership must impart a sense of mission and cyber exceptionalism within a cyber program at a given firm. Take my advice and build that spirit of cyber exceptionalism (Chapter "Cyber Exceptionalism") – the cyber security team will respond positively.

Given the existential threat from advanced threat vectors and the need for longer tenured security talent, I also recommend that CISOs make the case for long term retention bonuses or incentives for all security staff. If we need our top security talent to stay longer and provide that continuity required to defeat APT, then we must be ready to make longer term investment into them.

6 My Own Experience

I have successfully countered many cyber security engineers, architects, and managers in my time as a leader. Not once have I taken any punitive action against them at a later stage. In fact, most of them continued to have had long careers at that given firm.

Have people left after accepting my counteroffer? Yes, they have. Have folks resigned expecting a counter in the hope of getting a pay raise or promotion? Yes, they did, and they often did not receive a counteroffer.

Have I ever accepted a counteroffer in more than a quarter of a century of working? Yes, I have, with no regrets.

7 The CISO Take

The decision to accept (and offer) a counteroffer is situational and must be made in the context of the firm you work for, the work you do, your existing role, and your relationship with the team and the management. Rather than following any conventional rule of thumb, develop a clear-eyed view of the circumstances and use good judgment. Determine the levels of trust between you and your existing management, and gauge actual career and financial advancement opportunities available to you in your current situation to make the decision that is best for your personal and professional growth and development.

The CISOs really value their team members and will do their best to ensure that their staff is paid the market rate. Due to the delays in hiring a replacement, the risk to a company's security posture is too high if we cannot retain our talent due to our inability to pay the market rate.

Having said that, the CISOs would also be the first to admit that in some cases they cannot offer a counter offer due to financial constraints or in some cases they know that a change in job would really be beneficial for the career development and growth of the employee in question.

Going from personal experience, we had an employee that we had developed over the last 5 years leave us – he started as an entry-level engineer but became an indispensable member of our team during his next 5 years with us, and while we were sad to see him leave, we were very excited for the (bigger scope of) work that he would be doing at his future employer. He needed that experience for his future development, something that we could not give him at the current time. We parted ways knowing that he would take our culture and work ethic with him, with the hope that one day our paths will cross again.

Further Reading

Change (2020) Why You Should and Should not Accept a Counteroffer. https://www.changerecruit-mentgroup.com/knowledge-centre/why-you-should-and-should-not-accept-a-counteroffer. Accessed 18 Feb 2021

Niznik JS (2019) How to Decide if You Should Accept a Counteroffer. https://www.thebalanceca-reers.com/deciding-to-accept-or-decline-counteroffer-2070930. Accessed 18 Feb 2021

Badhwar (2021) The CISO's Next Frontier: AI, Post-Quantum Cryptography and Advanced Security Paradigms (Springer)

Importance of 1:1 Conversations

1 Introduction

Good communication with employees and team members within a cybersecurity program is one of the most important reasons for its success. One of the most important ways to keep employees engaged is the one-on-one conversation between an employee and his or her manager, whether they take place weekly, bi-weekly, or monthly. Rather than being an extended opportunity for managers to ask about project statuses, the agenda for one-on-one meetings between manager and employee should be set by the employee rather than the manager.

2 Guidance

I have provided some guidance in the chapter on some of the topics for discussion during these sessions. Our cybersecurity employees are key to the success of our company and I want to highlight that the leadership team is doing everything we can to ensure there is good communication between our managers and team members. As a CISO myself, I always seek this input to help me help my employees better.

2.1 What Is Going Well?

Talk about what is going well in your current role specifically or in your career generically.

© The Author(s), under exclusive license to Springer Nature
Switzerland AG 2021
R. Badhwar, *The CISO's Transformation*,
https://doi.org/10.1007/978-3-030-81412-0_17

Examples:

- I like this project I am on.
- I like the providing incident response and keeping data and systems safe.
- I like doing risk assessments.
- I like engineering new security systems and solutions.

2.2 What Is Not Going So Well?

Talk about what is not going so well in your current job or in your career in the recent past.
Examples:

- I worked over 75 h last week and have no work-life balance.
- I got paged five times last weekend and the one before.
- I am behind on my project deliverables due to operational responsibilities.
- I need technical help and guidance, but everyone else is too busy to help me.

2.3 Ask for Feedback

Ask for feedback from your current managers or team lead.
Examples:

- Can you please share feedback on my delivery on this project so far?
- Can you please share any feedback you may have any received from my peers within or outside the org?
- How can I be a better team player?

2.4 Give Feedback

Give feedback back to your manager on what they are doing better and where there may be opportunity for improvement.
Examples:

- During our 1:1's we talk more about projects and less about my career development. Can we change that?
- I don't think my skillset is being used to the fullest potential. Can you give me an opportunity to deliver on complex tasks?

2.5   Talk About Opportunities

Always talk to your manager about new(er) opportunities to pursue your interests or your personal development roadmap or career plan.
Examples:

- I want to work in Security Engineering.
- I want to move to the Incident response team.
- I want to work in Security Architecture.
- I want to do Security program management.
- I want to explore positions within Business IT teams.
- I want to mentor other junior engineers.

2.6   Talk About Career Growth

Talk to your manager about your career growth. Ask them for advice on what you need to do so that you can meet that career growth goal.
Examples:

- I want to follow a leadership career path.
- I'd like to get promoted this year as I am already delivering at the next level.
- I want to move back to a developer/engineer path (from management).

2.7   Talk About Individual Development

Always bring your individual development plan (IDP) to your 1:1 meeting with your manager or other senior leaders. Make sure it is discussed and any action items the manager took last time you met (e.g., finding some funding for training) are reviewed.
Example:

- I'd like to study for the CISSP certification. May I take a training course?
- I'd like to learn more about cyber threat mitigation techniques. May I attend Blackhat or Defcon?
- I'd like to pursue my master's degree. What are my options?

2.8 Brainstorm Ideas

Your manager was an engineer too at some time in her career, so if you have any ideas about product development or how you can help the team or company, then do speak about them. Maybe the company could patent that idea; maybe you can build or lead the development of a new product.

Examples:

- I know you are an expert in Firewalls, can you give me ideas on how to implement this new complex rule?
- I can implement SSO but can you help to federate an identity between AWS and Azure?

2.9 Skip Level Meetings

I recommend that in addition to weekly/bi-weekly meetings with your immediate manager or team lead, you also do quarterly skip level meetings with your manager's manager.

Skipping a management level could do either party a lot of good. The employee gets the bird's eye view of the senior manager and the senior manager listening to feedback from a person with whom they would not otherwise interact on a frequent basis.

Example:

- Can you please come to our staff meetings once a quarter and share your vision for our team from your vantage point?

3 The CISO Take

Frequent one-on-one meetings are very important to the success of a cybersecurity team. Cybersecurity professionals often only talk about security projects and security operations at the cost of discussing our professional development with our managers. It is very important for employees to reclaim this meeting time to provide feedback and solicit help with our professional development.

I also tried to highlight about what can one do to make these one-on-one meetings meaningful. While at work, people are generally stuck with the view from behind their desk, whether they have a very small view, or a very expansive view of what is happening within the company. While the majority of the work-day is spent in meetings discussing how to accomplish the work of the company, some types of meetings should be designated for sharing perspectives, so that the people doing the work are better understood and are better able to understand others.

Further Reading

Reynolds J (2016) The Importance of 1:1 Meetings – And What You Should Discuss in Them https://www.tinypulse.com/blog/-importance-of-11-meetings-and-what-you-should-discuss-in-them. Accessed 21 Feb 2021

Jones M (2020) 8 Tips and Best Practices on How to Train Employees for Cyber Security https://www.coxblue.com/8-tips-and-best-practices-on-how-to-train-employees-for-cyber-security/. Accessed 21 Feb 2021

Knight R (2016) How to Make Your One-on-Ones with Employees More Productive https://hbr.org/2016/08/how-to-make-your-one-on-ones-with-employees-more-productive. Accessed 21 Feb 2021

Badhwar (2021) The CISO's Next Frontier: AI, Post-Quantum Cryptography and Advanced Security Paradigms (Springer)

The Cyber Hygiene Mantra

1 Introduction

Recently, the Security Intelligence Handbook (Third Edition) published by Recorded Future stated that "**More threats are leveraging the same small set of vulnerabilities**" [2].

This statement is only partially true. It is true that more threats are leveraging the same small set of *commonly known* security vulnerabilities that should have been patched long ago. However, security leaders and their teams must also be concerned about threats leveraging a large number of *lesser known* and *even not yet identified* security vulnerabilities and weaknesses, whether in Web, Mobile, IVR, Chat Bots, Endpoint, Servers, or various other domains. These vulnerabilities can be exploited at any time and must be patched or mitigated with utmost urgency. The set of tools available to our red teams – Nmap, Shodan, Kali Linux/Metasploit, Ghidra, and CVE database– are also available to the attackers, who use them to identify the unpatched vulnerabilities that exist in your high risk, internet-exposed assets and systems. They can then either find (existing) exploits or write new ones for those vulnerabilities or "open" services. On top of this problem, there are the "insiders" or the malware that can exploit any vulnerabilities on your internal systems or network.

Every security technologist is trying to identify and patch these known vulnerabilities and ensure that they stay patched, since new vulnerability variations (and exploits) come out very frequently. Everyone is also working hard to develop the IOCs and other patterns to detect Zero-day and other attacks.

© The Author(s), under exclusive license to Springer Nature Switzerland AG 2021
R. Badhwar, *The CISO's Transformation*,
https://doi.org/10.1007/978-3-030-81412-0_18

2   Recommendation

Let's face it, dealing with vulnerabilities is a way of life for us. To reduce the probability of known and unknown exploited vulnerabilities, security teams can follow the Cyber Hygiene Mantra, elaborated here:

2.1   Identify and Patch All High/Medium Risk Vulnerabilities

(a) **Patch Away** – Patch all the known internal and external high and medium risk vulnerabilities to limit that threat vector.
(b) **Harden** all your internet-exposed and other high-risk internal assets and systems.
(c) **Hunt** – Don't trust only the security researchers or product vendors to find the vulnerabilities, at the exclusion of other valuable human resources. Instead, put your red and blue teams to work and have them use the same toolset available to the bad guys to proactively identify and highlight these vulnerabilities. Your red and blue teams can use Nmap, Shodan, Kali Linux/Metasploit, Ghidra, and CVE database, and the engineering teams can patch the vulnerabilities they find. A bug bounty program can also be helpful, especially for product companies.
(d) **IOCs (Indicators of Compromise)** – Use a cyber deception system combining Honeypot + Honeynet on steroids to gather intel on the threat actors and their techniques, and to create IOCs that you can feed to your IPS/IDS systems.
(e) **Threat Intel** – Obtain threat intel from public, private, and government sources (e.g., CISA, DHS, FS-ISAC, Civil Defense [UK]) to identify threat patterns. Use user entity behavior analysis (UEBA) at the endpoint and network to leverage the same IOCs (identified in (d)) to identify threat patterns and actors. Have an insider threat program to detect and mitigate data exfil, lateral movement and other internal threats.
(f) **Monitor and Respond.** Maintain a good monitoring and response program to provide real-time monitoring and incident response capabilities.

2.2   Reduce Threat Surface

(a) **Email Security** – Improve email security (e.g., implement a secure email gateway) to eliminate phishing and spoofing. Immediately implement DMARC. Also run continuous training and awareness campaigns to focus on detecting phishing and spoofing emails, among other things. Implementation of other techniques to "rewrite" URLs embedded within email, or open them in isolated (sandboxed) browsers, can also help mitigate zero day situations from advanced malware or defeat other techniques like drive-by-download.

(b) **Data Security** – Digitally protect all your data using digital rights management. Use a combination of data encryption and masking for your structured and unstructured business-sensitive and privacy data.

(c) **Network security** – Implement Zero Trust with least privilege. I know it's easier said than done, but if done right, it can lead you to network security nirvana. The technologies are now there to implement full macro- and micro network segmentation, and application segmentation. Also, harden your legacy network protocols like DNS (to DNSSEC) and NTP (to NTPSEC).

(d) **Cloud Security** – Implement full micro-segmentation. Encrypt all data at rest and in transit. Federate your identities. Use MFA for everything. Implement stringent access management controls. Use the dev-sec-ops paradigm with well-managed change control for CI/CD pipelines with full separations of roles and responsibilities, and vaulting of all privileged access accounts.

(e) **Endpoint and Network Visibility** – Ensure that ALL outbound traffic is encrypted and goes through your proxies. Have the capability to inspect all ingress and egress network traffic and look for patterns for malware and other security use cases (e.g., DLP). Have the capability to perform entity behavior analysis on endpoints (including mobile devices). Combine user and network entity behavior analysis along with data in your SIEM and run it by your AI algorithms for threat patterns that are otherwise hard to detect.

2.3 Perform Identity and Access Management

(a) **Identity Proofing** – All identities must be proofed using out of band (OOB) proofing techniques coupled with dynamic knowledge-based articles (KBA), before you create a record for them and give them validity and birthright.

(b) **Least Privilege** – Ensure proper access management to get to the least privilege paradigm for all your users, partners, and vendors (especially for users with escalated privileges, e.g., domain admins).

(c) **Privileged Credentials** – All privileged and admin credentials must be vaulted (and not hard coded or stored locally in configuration files).

(d) **MFA** – Use MFA enabled by a real authenticator. (These are cheap and commonly available.) Also use biometric authentication, such as fingerprints, face-id, or voice, whenever feasible.

(e) **Internet Facing** – Use MFA for all your (high-risk) internet-facing systems. Grant no exceptions!

(f) **Internal Facing** – Use MFA with adaptive authentication. Use step-up authentication for internal SSO paradigms.

2.4   Enable Asset Protection

(a) **Harden and Encrypt.** All endpoint assets should be hardened. Enable whole disk encryption to data security, along with safe boot to prevent any UEFI malware. All server assets should be hardened. Use whole disk encryption for any locally attached storage. All network-based storage such as SAN or NAS should be encrypted and scanned for malware.

(b) **Dynamic Whitelisting** – Make use of application control techniques like whitelisting to reduce malware and other harmful security attacks by only allowing approved and trusted (i.e., digitally signed) files, applications, and processes to be installed and run on a system (endpoint, server, or otherwise). The modern way of doing this is to use real-time dynamic whitelisting (although we should start using bias free lexicon like allowlist instead of whitelist).

(c) **Eliminate supply chain attacks.** Ensure that the most commonly used and statistically vulnerable software (e.g., Windows {no pun intended}) is always patched via gold images tested in lower-level environments. Also, pre-test all application or OS patches and only use windows tools (e.g., SCCM) to perform the patching on windows. Other tools that can (also) patch other platforms can also come in handy.

(d) **Reduce reliance on third-party patches** as much as possible.

(e) **Have advanced quarantine capability** for all end-user devices (including but not limited to laptops, tablets and smart phones) to stop malware infestation once detected.

2.5   Perform User Training and Awareness

(a) **Users can be the strongest or the weakest links** in the security chain. Make sure you have a user training and awareness program to keep them trained and well informed about security threats. Don't patronize them or blame them when they fail a phishing test. Train them and educate them to make sure they are the strong links they can be.

2.6   Setup a Certification and Accreditation (C&A) Program

I recommend that the CISOs setup a certification and accreditation (C&A) program to enable the capability to (continuously) assess resident cyber risk within an IT eco system, certify that the applications have the appropriate security controls implemented to bring the risk to an acceptable level, and provide an accreditation for the said certification through tracked artifacts in a GRC tool. Any applications that fail the certification or have expired accreditations are also tracked and reported.

Although these accreditations are reviewed and approved by the CISO on a continuous basis they also need the acceptance of other Senior or Executive leadership team members and thus any risk accepted by the business by running unaccredited applications puts the accountability also on them and just not on the CISO.

Do keep in mind that the CISO should never accept any security risk, their job is to remediate or mitigate the cyber risk. All cyber risks due to unpatched vulnerabilities or lack of investment into application or infrastructure modernization or into cybersecurity programming, needs to be accepted by the Head of the Business, the CIO, CRO or ultimately the CEO [1].

3 The CISO Take

Advanced threats are getting more sophisticated and persistent with every passing day. My recommendation is that CISOs take active personal interest in ensuring that the recommendations I have provided above for the six work-streams are actively heeded.

CISOs must also make the case for said cyber hygiene protocols to the board of directors, other executive business and C-Level leaders to ensure the appropriate prioritization and funding.

4 Definitions

CISA – stands for Cybersecurity and Infrastructure Security Agency. It is the nation's risk advisor, working with (public, private, corporate, non-profit and other government entities) partners to defend against today's threats and collaborating to build more secure and resilient infrastructure for the future [3].

DHS – stands for Department of Homeland Security. It is responsible for national security and has supervision over many areas, including cyber security and disaster recovery.

DMARC – stands for Domain-based Message Authentication Reporting and Compliance. It is an open email authentication protocol that enables domain-level protection of the email channel. It leverages DNS and uses the sender policy framework (SPF) and DomainKeys identified mail (DKIM) protocols to verify email senders. It authenticates legitimate email messages for email-sending domains and instructs on how to treat messages that fail authentication via policy settings.

IPS – stands for intrusion prevention system. It is a network security tool that provides monitoring (detection) and protection against network-based attacks and intrusions, including lateral movement.

MFA – stands for multi-factor authentication. It is an authentication technique used to grant access to a restricted resource (such as an application, system, website, or device) only after the user requesting the access has successfully presented two or more factors of information asserting possession (what a user has) and inherence (who a user is) to an authenticator.

NAS – stands for network attached storage. It is a single storage device that can be connected to a server or host over an ethernet network.

NTPSEC – stands for network time protocol secure.

SAN – stands for storage area network. It is composed of a network of storage devices that use block-based data.

SCCM – stands for System Center Configuration Manager. It is a Microsoft utility that provides the capability to administer and manage a large number of domain-attached windows-based computers. The services within the SCCM suite include patch management, OS deployment, and remote control, among others [3].

UEBA – stands for User and Entity Behavior Analytics. It uses machine learning algorithms to analyze large datasets collected from user endpoints and/or servers to model and create baselines of typical and atypical behaviors of humans and machines within a network [3].

UEFI – stands for Unified Extensible Firmware Interface. Eventually expected to replace the BIOS, it is the first program that executes when a computer is turned on. Simply speaking, it is a secure rewrite of the BIOS and provides the specifications to enable a secure way for the computer's firmware to connect with its operating system (OS).

References

1. Moore S (2020) Gartner Predicts 75% of CEOs Will be Personally Liable for Cyber-Physical Security Incidents by 2024 https://www.gartner.com/en/newsroom/press-releases/2020-09-01-gartner-predicts-75%2D%2Dof-ceos-will-be-personally-liabl. Accessed Jan 5 2021.
2. The Recorded Future Team (2020) How Security Intelligence Enables Risk-Prioritized Vulnerability Management. https://www.recordedfuture.com/vulnerability-management-prioritization/, Accessed 6 Dec 2020
3. Badhwar (2021) The CISO's Next Frontier: AI, Post-Quantum Cryptography and Advanced Security Paradigms (Springer)

Further Reading

Cybersecurity and Infrastructure Security Agency. https://www.cisa.gov/ Accessed 6 Dec 2020
Department of Homeland Security (2020) Cybersecurity and Critical Infrastructure. https://www.dhs.gov/coronavirus/cybersecurity-and-critical-infrastructure Accessed 6 Dec 2020
Civil Defense today. UK. https://www.civildefence.co.uk/ Accessed 6 Dec 2020
Cybersecurity and Infrastructure Security Agency (2020) About CISA. https://www.cisa.gov/about-cisa Accessed 6 Dec 2020
Ministry of Home Affairs, Government of India. Civil Defense. https://dgfscdhg.gov.in/civil-defence Accessed 6 Dec 2020

Microsoft (2020). Boot to UEFI Mode or legacy BIOS mode. https://docs.microsoft.com/en-us/windows-hardware/manufacture/desktop/boot-to-uefi-mode-or-legacy-bios-mode Accessed 6 Dec 2020

Wikipedia (2021). DoD Information Assurance Certification and Accreditation Process (DIACAP). https://en.wikipedia.org/wiki/Department_of_Defense_Information_Assurance_Certification_and_Accreditation_Process Accessed March 11, 2021.

CyberArk (2020) Privileged Access Management (PAM) https://www.cyberark.com/what-is/privileged-access-management/ Accessed April 15, 2021.

Microsoft (2020) Store credential in Azure Key Vault https://docs.microsoft.com/en-us/azure/data-factory/store-credentials-in-key-vault Accessed April 15. Accessed April 15, 2021.

Part III
Cybersecurity Prudence

Cybersecurity Lessons from the Breach of Physical Security at US Capitol Building

1 Introduction

The cyber security code of ethics is not just to protect our systems and data, but also to protect the society, the commonwealth, and the infrastructure, and to act honorably, honestly, responsibly, and justly. We shall stay vigilant when we see any activity (cyber or otherwise) that goes against our code.

I am deeply saddened by the assault on the US Capitol building and our democracy in our nation's capital by a violent mob of rioters on January 6, 2021 [1]. I condemn these attacks and hope the rioters will be brought to justice.

In the cyber security context, we are all too familiar with threat actors, trying to create a façade so that they can carry on other malicious activities, but it our job to be vigilant and stand firm to our mission.

2 Best Practices

While the physical components of this attack are apparent, there are also some relevant cyber security lessons that we can use to protect our own office locations –

Whole disk (or Volume) encryption – from the reports published, the attackers gained inappropriate access to or stole laptops and other devices that either belonged to members of congress or their staffers. This highlights the need for whole disk encryption (enabled by BitLocker in windows, and MDM/MAM on mobile devices) which encrypts all the data on a drive and prevents it from any unauthorized viewing, copying, or exfiltration. This will also provide protection from other malicious attempts like jail breaking or root kitting on a stolen device.

Remote Wipe – for reasons mentioned above, the capability to remotely wipe (or destroy) the data resident on the stolen devices and computers needs to exist. An

© The Author(s), under exclusive license to Springer Nature Switzerland AG 2021
R. Badhwar, *The CISO's Transformation*,
https://doi.org/10.1007/978-3-030-81412-0_19

information security team can remotely wipe all the laptops that may have been either stolen or compromised. The devices must also enable location services, so that these devices can be remotely tracked and (pre-emptively) wiped when necessary.

Network Access Control (NAC) – This capability manages the device (and user) access to private networks primarily through the enforcement of authentication and authorization controls. The rioters had physical access to network jacks and other computing gear in the capitol building and may have installed rogue network listening and sniffing devices. With a NAC implementation, these rogue devices would not be allowed to connect to the local network, preventing them from gaining unauthorized access into the local network or listening in on any data being transmitted through the network. This would also prevent the technique used by malicious entities and attackers to use a rogue wireless access point (AP) to stand up a fake local wireless (Wi-Fi) network in their attempt to phish an institution's network or application credentials or to route that institution's network traffic through a malicious proxy.

Biometric Recognition – The capability needs to exist to recognize the attackers (or imposters) from their biometric features. This is generally done using facial recognition capability, but other biometric attributes like voice can also be used to recognize these attackers from their social media profiles, and video and voice recording either made during the attack or at other occasions.

Security Hygiene – This highlights the need for commonsense and basic security hygiene, such as the usage of secure passwords for laptops and mobile devices. I recommend that a password of at least 15 characters be used for windows or network logins, and a pin of at least eight digits for mobile devices. In addition, wherever possible, please consider the usage of biometric authentication to enable multi-factor authentication (MFA) before access is granted to a laptop or phone.

Local Network Closet Protection – Although data centers are generally very well protected, most local sites have network closets that house local networking gear (e.g., switches, hubs, routers and local firewalls) that are readily accessible. These must be properly secured to be made tamper-proof. All local network closets must either be resident in a tamper-proof cage or in a room secured with biometric authentication and video monitoring.

Local Video monitoring – All local sites must use video monitoring for all common and secure areas. In case a site is overrun by a rioting mob, the cybersecurity security operations center (SOC) must have visibility to the site, so that they can immediately implement any remote protection measures, including but not limited to calling law enforcement, remote pre-emptive wiping of critical devices, or remote lockdown of office segments.

Collaboration – Cyber security personnel need to work with our physical security peers and maintain a secure state and perimeter. To quote Aesop, 'United we stand, or divided we shall fall.'

Also, according to Gartner "By 2025, 50% of asset-intensive organizations will converge their cyber, physical and supply chain security teams under one chief security officer role that reports directly to the CEO" [2], and thus is there an opportunity across the board to bring both cyber and physical security under the leadership of the CISO to further optimize the program and improve our capabilities to provide better incident response to attacks whether they be cyber or physical.

Threat hunting – In case a breach does occur, then the capability must exist to examine any malicious behavior or anomalous activity to detect any compromise of an endpoint or a network component. This is generally achieved by having endpoint discovery and response capability on the endpoint, and pattern recognition capability within the network traffic itself to look for lateral movement, insider threats, and any DNS or TCP/UDP traffic destined for command and control (CnC) servers. Capability must also exist to perform threat hunting as part of the company's incident response capability, where they can hunt for compromised assets, and either block or quarantine them.

3 The CISO Take

Cyber and physical security teams have operated separately since they became distinct mainstream entities. Many of them operate their own security operations centers (SOC) and tooling. Given the state of civil unrest and rioting in various cities around the world, the threat scenario poses challenges of equal importance to physical and cyber security alike. The use of physical attack or brute force to infiltrate offices and data centers, to steal important hardware and devices or to install network sniffers and malicious access points (AP) should compel cyber and physical security teams to join forces and work as one team under the leadership of the CISO to provide better protection from these types of threats.

The sophistication of cyber security tooling, access to threat intelligence and advanced alerts, and event correlation capabilities available with the SIEM, combined with the acumen of the physical security team with their law enforcement experience, can all contribute to the formation of a formidable security team that can handle these new threats that pose significant risk to our enterprises.

4 Definitions

CnC – stands for command and control (server). Generally, a cloud-hosted server/ system often working in tandem with the usage of DGA-generated domains, the CnC is used by threat actors to control and manage infected and breached endpoints and servers (generally resident) on private networks [3].

DNS – stands for Domain Name System. It is a global naming system which enables the mapping and the subsequent syncing of a website or other internet/intranet-hosted resource name, to an IP address.

Jailbreaking – It is the technique to gain unauthorized access to a computing device by exploiting flaws in the operating system or bios to install (unsigned or untrusted) software (malicious or otherwise) and override any restrictions implemented by the device manufacturer. It allows the attacker to gain administrative (root) access to the operating system and access all the device or system features.

MAM – stands for mobile application management. It provides the capability to enable security controls for specific (corporate) applications and their related data instead of the entire device. Generally, this is done by installing management software on the device, which provides the company's information security team the remote management capability to lockdown, track, and wipe just the corporate application and related data. Modern MAM solutions can also integrate with digital rights management solutions (e.g., AIP), further improving the data security posture of a company on BYOD devices.

MDM – stands for Mobile Device Management. It provides the capability to securely manage mobile devices (and even laptops) by securing the device, itself. Generally, this is done by installing a management software on the device which enables whole disk encryption to protect that data within the MDM "container" from unauthorized access and exfiltration. It also provides the company's information security team the remote management capability to lockdown, track, and wipe the employee's corporate issued mobile device.

MFA – stands for multi factor authentication. It is an authentication technique used to grant access to a restricted resource (application, system, website, device etc.) only after the user requesting the access has successfully presented two or more factors of information asserting possession (what a user has) and inherence (who a user is) to an authenticator.

Rootkit – is generally used to refer to the malicious firmware/software tools used to gain unauthorized access to the administrative (root) account of a computing system or device.

SOC – stands for Security Operations Center. The SOC represents the combined capabilities provided by security professionals (generally resident in a secured physical space), processes and technologies with a mission to provide 24 × 7 security, network and application monitoring services for a given enterprise [3].

References

1. Wikipedia (2021). The 2021 storming of the United States Capitol https://en.wikipedia.org/wiki/2021_storming_of_the_United_States_Capitol. Accessed Feb 20, 2021
2. Olyaei S, Thielemann K et al (2021). Predicts 2021: Cybersecurity Program Management and IT Risk Management. Accessed Feb 20, 2021
3. Badhwar (2021) The CISO's Next Frontier: AI, Post-Quantum Cryptography and Advanced Security Paradigms (Springer)

Further Reading

Gewirtz D (2021). Capitol attack's cybersecurity fallout: Stolen laptops, lost data and possible espionage https://www.zdnet.com/article/capitol-attacks-cybersecurity-fallout-stolen-laptops-lost-data-and-possible-espionage/ Accessed Feb 20, 2021.

Paul K (2021). Theft of two computers during Capitol attack raises information security concerns. https://www.theguardian.com/us-news/2021/jan/08/capitol-attack-computer-theft-information-security Accessed Feb 20, 2021.

Rosenblatt S (2021). US Capitol attack a wake-up call for the integration of physical & IT security https://www.darkreading.com/physical-security/us-capitol-attack-a-wake-up-call-for-the-integration-of-physical-and-it-security/d/d-id/1339869 Accessed Feb 20, 2021.

Protect Society, the Commonwealth, and the Infrastructure – Post COVID-19

1 Introduction

The first canon within the (ISC)² code of ethics asks the Certified Information Systems Security Professional (CISSP) certification holders to "Protect society, the commonwealth, and the infrastructure." While the primary mission of the CISO, other cyber-security professionals, and CISSPs is to provide for the security of a given company's data, system, and infrastructure, their training makes them adept at creating out-of-the-box solutions to societal problems that may directly or indirectly cause loss of human life, like this current pandemic that we all are trying to deal with.

2 Technical Controls Required to Securely Work from Home, and Back

I have written extensively about the various cyber security controls that need to be implemented to enable the capability to work securely in a COVID-19 (caused by SARS-CoV-2) induced extended work-from-home paradigm. Below I am going to share some thoughts about the common sense non-cyber-security steps a security professional would take to get back to work using some cyber-security infused constructs – so please bear with me.

© The Author(s), under exclusive license to Springer Nature
Switzerland AG 2021
R. Badhwar, *The CISO's Transformation*,
https://doi.org/10.1007/978-3-030-81412-0_20

3 Number of Masks Required to Securely Go Back to Work

Security people are in the business of managing risk. We always like to remediate the risk, if we can't then we try to mitigate the risk, and when nothing else works then we try to assume the risk as a last resort for a manageable period while still trying to find ways to better deal with it.

Now that we have successfully managed to mitigate most of the security risk from 99% of our workforce working from home for a fairly extended period, it is now time for us to plan our move back to our work locations in a phased manner. Given that the virus is still being transmitted and has not been eradicated, again we have to think about how best to manage the residual risk. The way to remediate this risk would be seasonal vaccination (like we do with the flu) once the newly available vaccine shots have been given to every citizen that wants them. In the meantime, we have to try to mitigate this risk. There are many good ideas about mitigating this risk (e.g., like wrist bands to help maintain social distancing and thermal scanners at work to measure elevated temperatures) and I am going to share one such basic idea that I think may also work well.

It has been hypothesized that if a person A was infected with COVID-19 and were to be in proximity of another person B, then the probability of B getting infected is less than 5% if both were to follow proper hygiene protocols such as hand-washing, wearing an (N-95 or equivalent) mask and gloves and maintaining a reasonable physical distance from one another (aka, social-distancing) [1–3]. We security technologists generally develop and implement extremely complex systems, but sometimes a basic idea can help mitigate the risk at hand. In spite of the simplicity of the solutions, logistical issues still make them difficult to implement. Let's do the math: we have about 328 M people in the United States. Let's assume that one third of the population, about 100 M people, have to go out to earn a living. The working population will need masks. Since these masks are generally single use, assuming we can wear the same mask for one entire day (which is a bit of a stretch), we would need 30x100M = 3B masks per month, or approximately 10B masks for the next few months once we open. While it is a large number of masks, we should be able to implement this mitigating control. Until we either develop herd immunity or get vaccinated, we have to employ simple yet effective solutions to keep our lives and livelihood intact.

4 Virus Tracking (SARS-CoV-2)

Cybersecurity technologists have perfected the art of detecting and tracking computer viruses by creating hashes, which are unique signatures, and indicators of compromise (IOCs), which are observed behavioral traits characteristic of a computer virus. In organizational settings, we make this information readily available as threat Intel and share it across our ecosystems in an attempt to collaborate and protect ourselves from malware infestations. I believe we need the same capability and speed in tracking biological viruses, by providing better technological capabilities to the World Health Organization (WHO) and other national governments.

Currently most of the SARS-CoV-2 tracking is haphazard for the various local variants that have been discovered over the last 1 year. Although WHO is tracking the virus, many countries are not participating. Even within a country like the United States, a lot of the tracking is being done at a state level.

Let's talk about general biological virus detection first. Among all the various tests in the medical world, the test that is most frequently used is something called 'Rapid Influenza Diagnostic Test' (RIDT) for the influenza virus, which looks for viral antigens in the specimen with very rudimentary capability to detect the viral types and mutations. Most of this testing is chemical based where a reaction causes a color to change for a positive test. RDITs are not very accurate. There are other more accurate tests like Molecular Assays, some of which can provide better capability to detect the viral strain and mutation, but even these are based on chemical reactions which detect antibodies, rather than the DNA of the virus. That is the reason why tests often inadequately detect the flu or other viral infections, especially if the virus has mutated and the regular antigen/antibody based (chemical reaction) test programmed for a different strain does not work.

What we need is to create a cryptographic hash for the genetic structure of the virus in question. This can be done by storing the DNA or RNA sequence of the virus, to create a hash one would need to break down the nucleotides that actually store the genetic information i.e., adenine (A), cytosine (C), guanine (G) and thymine (T). Please note that the viruses may be structurally very simple but have complex genetic material – they may either have DNA (double-stranded) or RNA (single-stranded) genetic material. The virus genome uses the same genetic coding (e.g., A, C, G, T) as living human and animal cells, or else they would not be able to reprogram their host cells to multiply.

One could easily use existing hashing algorithms i.e., SHA256, SHA384 or SHA512 to perform the hashing since all these algorithms can take in an input of variable size and spit out a unique and uniform hash without any collisions. Also, one could further customize these hashing algorithms to develop a unique hashing scheme (algorithm) designed specifically for DNA sequences. Once a unique hash has been created, it can then be loaded to an open blockchain-enabled system that can be used to share information worldwide as a source of an open yet immutable data repository to track every virus and their mutations known to mankind that have been sequenced in a lab. This large dataset can then be analyzed by machine learning algorithms to gain useful insight that will come in handy in cure creation and prevention.

The reason the medical world uses chemical-reaction based tests is because they are fast and cheap. With the advent of supercomputers, cloud-based distributed computing, machine learning infused data science, and with the possibility of quantum computing, the theoretical algorithmic capability that already exists to sequence the genetic structure from every patient for any viral and bacterial infection can be further augmented by the exponential increase in computing capability. This would provide us great capability to provide fault tolerant ways of detecting viruses and their mutations, and tracking down patient zero for every mutation worldwide.

With such detailed understanding, medication and prevention measures could be effectively tailored to unique information about a virus and its variants.

5   The CISO Take

I know I crossed the cyber-security domain boundary into medical science, but I humbly believe that what we have learned and implemented in the cyber and information technology world can be reused. We can defeat this pandemic with the doctors, scientists and the medical services professionals leading the charge, but they can certainly use all the help the Information and Cybersecurity technologists can provide them to better detect and track these pandemic viruses, in order to find and tailor the needed cures.

If nothing else I hope at least some of you found this to be intriguing.

6   Definitions

CISSP – Certified Information Systems Security Professional. Is a security certification granted by (ISC)^2.

Cryptographic hash – is an algorithm that takes input data of variable size (message) and converts it into an output array of fixed size (generally called message digest or hash).

ISC^2 – Is an international, nonprofit membership association for information security leaders. It offers many certifications including but not limited to CISSP.

SHA – stands for secure hashing algorithm. It is a family of cryptographic (one way) data hashing or obfuscation algorithms that have been approved for use by the National Institute of Standards and Technology (NIST). SHA1 has been deemed as breached and has been deprecated. SHA2 (i.e., 256, 384, 512) and SHA3 family of functions are approved for use.

Further Reading

Guarino B, Janes C et al (2020) Spate of new research supports wearing masks to control coronavirus spread. https://www.washingtonpost.com/health/2020/06/13/spate-new-research-supports-wearing-masks-control-coronavirus-spread/. Accessed 05 Dec 2020

CDC (2020) Guidance for Wearing Masks Help Slow the Spread of COVID-19 https://www.cdc.gov/coronavirus/2019-ncov/prevent-getting-sick/cloth-face-cover-guidance.html. Accessed 05 Dec 2020

(ISC)2 https://www.isc2.org/

Chu D, Akl E, et al (2020) Physical distancing, face masks, and eye protection to prevent person-to-person transmission of SARS-CoV-2 and COVID-19: a systematic review and meta-analysis. https://www.thelancet.com/article/S0140-6736(20)31142-9/fulltext, Accessed 05 Dec 2020

Godfried I (2020) Machine Learning methods to aid in Coronavirus Response https://towards-datascience.com/machine-learning-methods-to-aid-in-coronavirus-response-70df8bfc7861 Accessed 05 Feb 2021

Badhwar (2021) The CISO's Next Frontier: AI, Post-Quantum Cryptography and Advanced Security Paradigms (Springer)

Self-Service Recovery Options for Bricked Windows Devices

1 Introduction

In this chapter, I am going to provide some basic, common sense guidance on how to recover your Windows device if it fails to boot, or if it gets the "blue screen of death" (BSOD) or, as some would put it – gets bricked.

Some may ask, why is a CISO providing basic guidance? I have two responses to that. First, although I have been a security leader for some of the largest corporations in the world, I am still an engineer at heart, as well as a friend, a father, a brother, a son, and a son-in-law. While my immediate family may be up-to-speed on some of these items, the many pings I have received from others suggest that many people are not. Secondly, a laptop may have been bricked due to a **security issue** and while there are (professional) remedies available to folks at their work locations, they may still need help for their personal assets at home. Also, no question is too stupid and no solution too basic, if it can help someone reduce some cyber risk or bring some peace of mind. Sometimes the simplest solution is the best solution.

2 Solutions

There are various reasons for a given Windows (10) device to get the BSOD or encounter total boot failure (aka bricked). It could be due to **malware**, a Windows application software security (patch) update incompatible with hardware or other software on your particular machine, newly installed software, or a hardware failure or malfunction.

If we recognize the likelihood of a device getting bricked before it happens to us, we can proactively safeguard our home laptops or desktops; otherwise, the

R. Badhwar, *The CISO's Transformation*, https://doi.org/10.1007/978-3-030-81412-0_21

post-bricking recovery options are fewer, harder and, in relying on services such as Geek Squad, much costlier.

Here are three fundamental things that each and every one of us **must do immediately and repeat on a periodic basis**, if we own a windows desktop or laptop at home:

(a) Create a USB boot drive.
(b) Create a USB recovery drive, or media (DVD or CD).
(c) Create a weekly backup of your personal data and files on a secure, encrypted, and tamper-resistant drive.

2.1 USB Boot Drive

This is a generic windows boot drive which, once created, will be able to boot a Windows machine for versions of the Operating System (OS) still supported by Microsoft (e.g., Windows 10). This can get complicated with the new Windows 10 release model (LTSB/LTSC and CBB/Semi-Annual channel), but that is outside the scope of this introductory discussion at the current time.

You can only be successful in creating this generic boot drive while the Windows machine is operational. (We will cover the other edge cases later in this chapter.)

Check your access to the Windows advanced boot menu by hitting the F8 key. If hitting the F8 key brings you to the advanced boot menu, then it would come in handy if your device were to brick. Note that Windows 10 has a Fast Boot capability, which makes it extremely difficult to get to the boot menu outside the OS. You need to press the F8 key within 200 milliseconds of restarting or powering up a machine. However, there are steps you can take which will allow you to press the F8 key within a more reasonable 1 s timeframe, as if you were working within a pre-Windows 10 legacy configuration. These are the steps to take:

1. Bring yourself to the F8 Advanced Boot Options screen by typing the following command from the windows 'cmd' prompt as administrator (The cmd as administrator can be found by typing cmd in the windows 'search of anything' box in the bottom left corner):

   bcdedit / set {bootmgr} displaybootmenu yes

2. Assuming you already have Windows 10 installed and licensed, you must then download the 'Create Windows 10 Installation Media' and run the 'Microsoft Media Creation Tool' [1].
3. Connect a USB drive with a minimum 16 GB of available space. You can also create a DVD, in which you would need a DVD drive with R/W (reading and writing) capability. *Please note that the media creation tool will wipe your USB drive clean before it creates the boot drive and thus you will lose any existing*

data. *Note that if you have been creating weekly backups, you should not have to worry about data loss.*

4. When you execute this tool, you must select the option to "Create Installation media (USB Flash Drive, DVD, or ISO file) for another PC." (Select the language {English}, Edition {Win 10}, Architecture {32 or 64 bit})
5. You can then either put the boot media on a USB drive, or an ISO file on a USB, which you then need to burn on a DVD. (The tool will probably run for 10 minutes.)
6. This boot drive can be used for any Windows 10 machine. (Note that a 32-bit boot drive will work for a 64-bit machine, but the reverse is not true.)

2.2 Create a USB Recovery Drive, or Media (DVD or CD)

1. On your Windows 10 device next to the Start button search for 'create a recovery drive.'
2. Run the 'Create the Recovery Drive' tool.
3. Connect a USB drive with minimum 32 GB of available space. Please note that the creation tool will wipe your USB drive clean before it creates the recovery drive and thus you will lose any existing data.
4. The tool will run for a while (30–45 minutes) and will create a recovery drive to be used ONLY for the PC on which it was made.

3 BSOD or Bricked?

When a device bricks, there are two recovery options: either boot the machine using the USB boot drive created before getting bricked or use the recovery drive. Here are the pros and cons of each option:

3.1 USB Boot Drive

(a) USB Boot drive is the preferred approach if the user has this pre-created and readily available.
(b) One USB boot drive will mostly work on other similar machines with similar versions of the OS.
(c) The boot drive may not be able to recover from failures caused either by hardware failure or by sophisticated malware or other serious operating system issues. (It generally can only recover from Boot sector corruption issues, which are often the handiwork of malware.)

(d) To use this option, the user needs to connect the USB Boot drive and restart the machine.

(e) Once recovered and logged in, the user may also need to repair their windows installation. (a) Select the 'reset this pc' within the 'update and security' settings section to completely fix the machine, which may include but not be limited to a complete OS reset; (b) In some cases, just running the Anti-Virus (AV) engine may be enough if the boot sector corruption was done by some malware, in which case you must remove all malware. (c) If you create a USB boot drive from an infected PC, then you must also run an AV scan on it.

3.2 Recovery Drive

(a) The recovery drive can recover from serious OS issues and malware infestations.

(b) The recovery drive needs to be pre-created and readily available for use when needed.

(c) This option does not need the Advanced F8 Boot option.

(d) If you use this option, you will lose ALL your personal data.

(e) The recovery drive only has the OS and other necessary system files but will **NOT** recover your personal data. This is why it is important to make a regular habit of backing up your data independent of such events. Your personal data may only be restored from such backups.

(f) To use this option, the user just needs to connect the USB drive and power the device.

3.3 Prerequisites

The user needs to ensure:

Access to the system configuration by pressing F10 when starting up the computer.

(a) UEFI boot order in the system configuration is in the following order: 1. OS Boot Manager 2. USB 3. CD/DVD 4. Network adapter.

(b) The legacy boot order is 1. Hard drive 2. USB 3. CD/DVD 4. Network adapter.

4 Edge Cases

1. If the legacy configuration for the Advanced F8 boot option (via command above) is not enabled, then the user must repeatedly press F8 at startup for windows to load the Boot menu. (This is not an easy task.)

2. If the user does not have a USB Boot drive or recovery drive, they must press F8 to try to boot in SAFE mode. (You do need the Advanced F8 boot option for this to work, so that you can get to the boot menu to get to SAFE mode.)
3. One other option available is to press F11 at restart time and then go to Troubleshoot > Advanced options > Startup Repair. or go to F8 from within that menu. (This may not be available for all and is manufacturer dependent.)

5 The CISO Take

Although these are basic instructions, they can prove very useful if/when your (or your mom's or dad's) personal Windows device bricks. Please **do not** try these for your work devices—let the security professionals do their jobs to recover those work machines.

This chapter also drives in the message about the breadth of the CISO role and the fact that they have to be ready for the possibility that a (basic) blue screen of death for (personal or work) windows machines may have been caused by a mal-ware infection and thus cannot be ignored.

6 Definitions

LTSB – stands for Long-Term Servicing Branch for Windows 10. It has now been replaced by LTSC.

LTSC – stands for Long-Term Servicing Channel. It is identical to old versions of Windows where users receive security updates and bug fixes every month, but no new features and enhancements are installed. The minimum length of servicing lifetime of LTSC is 10 years [2].

CBB – stands for Current Branch for Business for Windows 10. It has been replaced by the Semi-Annual-Channel.

Semi-Annual Channel - This is the latest version of Windows and is called Semi-Annual Channel (Targeted). This version receives all upgrades (new versions) and updates (patches) from Microsoft within a few days of their release [2].

UEFI – stands for Unified Extensible Firmware Interface. It is a specification for a software interface that connects a computer's operating system to its firmware.

References

1. Microsoft (2020) Software Download page. https://www.microsoft.com/en-us/software-download/windows10. Accessed 10 May 2020
2. Geelen P (2020) Windows 10 Servicing Branches (CB, CBB, and LTSB), Semi-Annual Channel. Available via Microsoft TechNet Wiki. https://social.technet.microsoft.com/wiki/contents/articles/33703.windows-10-servicing-branches-cb-cbb-and-ltsb-semi-annual-channel.aspx. Accessed 10 May 2020

Further Reading

Badhwar (2021) The CISO's Next Frontier: AI, Post-Quantum Cryptography and Advanced Security Paradigms (Springer)

Certification & Accreditation

1 Introduction

To protect company systems and applications, CISOs need to have a very good understanding of the cyber risk the company carries. The CISOs and the rest of the cybersecurity team need to devise a way to quantify this risk for all new systems before and after they are put into production. They can then manage, mitigate, and remediate this risk and provide visibility to executive management on the company's current state of risk by implementing security controls.

To quantify the cumulative cyber risk in a given IT portfolio, it is important that every existing or new IT application in the company be scanned for vulnerabilities and weaknesses. All applications should be analyzed to determine if they are running a current version of the software (i.e., no worse than N-2), to validate the security of any internal and external (third party) dependencies, and to verify that systems and applications are either regularly patched or getting OEM-issued security patches for known vulnerabilities and weaknesses. These measures ensure that mitigating and/or compensating controls are in place to prevent the exploitation of vulnerabilities, and to establish a timeline for vulnerability remediation.

While there are various ad-hoc ways to go about this exercise, I recommend that CISOs consider adopting the process of Certification and Accreditation (C&A). This process has been successfully used by many federal and civilian (government) agencies, and defense contractors that are part of the military industrial complex.

© The Author(s), under exclusive license to Springer Nature
Switzerland AG 2021
R. Badhwar, *The CISO's Transformation*,
https://doi.org/10.1007/978-3-030-81412-0_22

2 Making the Case

Although the traditional Certification and Accreditation (C&A) process was transformed into the six-step Risk Management Framework (RMF) as defined within the NIST Special Publication 800–37 – the guide for Applying the Risk Management Framework to Federal Information System [1], and has been adopted by many federal and National defense agencies (e.g. DOD, FBI, NSA, DISA, etc.), this chapter makes the case for using the same process for the security certification and accreditation of non-defense information systems for highly regulated industries or other industries that carry customer/client sensitive data. This process could be highly beneficial to insurance, banking, pharmaceutical, retirement, and asset management companies.

These guidelines as laid out in NIST 800-37, or even a simplified version of the same customized to the needs of a given company, provide approved technical and non-technical security controls and standards for a consistent, repeatable compliance assessment framework for information systems. Following the guidelines will protect sensitive company data and assets and thereby help establish the current security state baseline for the ecosystem.

This scheme as defined in NIST SP 800-37 can be simplified and used as a guide to create:

(a) A customized risk and security assessment process to certify that new applications comply with a given firm's information security policy and standards.
(b) A periodic risk and security reassessment process for all existing internet-facing and internal systems with high-risk vulnerabilities, or systems that need better protection due to the (sensitive) nature of the data they store.
(c) An exception granting process to allow unaccredited systems to operate while undergoing certification and accreditation (C&A).
(d) An exception granting process for unaccredited (transient or short life) systems that will never have C&A and will only operate in a limited capacity for a short period with least privilege (e.g., work done by audit firms like E&Y or PWC).
(e) A GRC tool (e.g., ServiceNow or Archer) to store all the assessment and compliance artifacts (i.e., ATOs and POA&Ms).
(f) A cybersecurity steering committee chaired by the CISO and made up of senior leaders, including the CIO, CRO, CLO, CPO, CDO, and LOB presidents. The committee would have the power to grant (ATO) approvals and exceptions.
(g) A program of company-wide security awareness training that includes information on the certification and accreditation process.
(h) Security reference architecture and patterns for high-risk system threat mitigation, incorporating other security best practices for efficiently repeating the C&A process.

3 The Workflow Outline

The simplified C&A workflow consists of the following phases:

3.1 Initiation Phase

In the initiation phase, the system requirements and application design are reviewed to find and correct any divergence from security design guidance and identify any noncompliance with existing security policy and standards.

The initial phase includes both (new) implementations and reassessments. New applications and systems can be scrutinized to catch any divergence from security standards before going live in production. Existing or legacy systems can undergo reassessment using current security standards. If legacy systems and applications don't have the requirements and design artifacts or don't meet current security standards, then the owners of those systems or applications would have to ask for an exception. Such systems and applications may only be allowed to operate in a restricted manner for a finite (agreed upon) period.

3.2 Security Certification Phase

This phase is used to verify and certify that, all the systems, applications (software and firmware) and operating systems in scope have been hardened and configured with guidance from applicable NIST or CIS hardening guidelines, and comply with existing security policy, standards and published patterns.

Some of the above-mentioned verification takes the form of vulnerability scans of application and systems software and shared libraries, static and dynamic code analysis, software composition analysis, network segmentation analysis, and (internal and external) penetration tests.

3.3 Security Accreditation Phase

Systems undergoing certification become accredited in this phase. This accreditation process involves the final reviews with the technology and business owners of the systems and applications.

One of the primary activities during this phase is the verification that any issues (vulnerabilities or weaknesses) or deviations identified during the certification phase have been remediated or that acceptable compensating or mitigating controls have been implemented to bring the residual risk or risk/severity rating to an acceptable level.

Once a final review has been completed, the CISO or an authorized delegate for the system generally grants an authorization to operate (ATO) to the System Technology or Business owner. Although this can vary from company to company, it is my recommendation that the period for which an ATO is granted should not exceed 1 year. I also recommend that an artifact for the given system describing its ATO status (accredited, unaccredited or accredited with exception) be recorded in a company standard GRC tool.

The accreditation with exception status is represented by providing an ATO with conditions (ATOC) and is generally only granted for shorter periods (30–90 days) in case there are minor issues that can be corrected within the stipulated time before a full ATO can be granted. If the (minor) issues are not resolved within the ATOC period, then the accreditation must be withdrawn and the status updated immediately in the GRC tool.

If an accreditation is withdrawn (as above) due an unresolved pending issue or the issuance of a new critical or high vulnerability, or if an ATO cannot be granted for functional, technical, procedural, or ownership issues or concerns, then generally the system owner is given 30–90 days to remediate the issues, resolve the problems, or submit an exception request along with a remediation plan generally referred to as plan of action and milestones (POA&M) to the Office of the CISO. The schedule to provide the corrective actions in the POA&M generally should not exceed 180 days.

The exception and POA&M must be presented to and approved by the CISO and the cyber security steering committee.

Having a valid and active ATO authorizes the deployment and operation of a given application in production. Although an ATO asserts that the application has been subjected to systematic evaluation in accordance with the company's security policy and hardening guidelines, it does not guarantee that a system may not get breached by advanced threats or infected by malware. From my experiences, the probability that an application with an active ATO gets breached is much lower than an application without an ATO.

Given the dynamic and evolving nature of the cyber threats, security teams generally reserve the right to withdraw the ATO for a given system if critical vulnerabilities are detected and are not remediated within an agreed upon time as stipulated by the CISO.

3.4   Continuous Monitoring Phase

In this phase, continuous monitoring of all the company systems with documented ATOs ensures their continued compliance with company policy and standards.

To engage in continuous monitoring, the CISO's security team reviews all the ATOs and POA&Ms. on a monthly basis; the cybersecurity steering committee reviews all ATOs and POA&Ms along with exception requests on a quarterly basis.

4 The CISO Take

Setting up a certification and accreditation (C&A) program can prove very beneficial for continuous cybersecurity program assessment. CISOs who work in the federal or defense sectors, or in other heavily regulated industries are generally required to have a C&A program in place.

The cost-benefit analysis of cyber/data breach losses vs. the loss from the additional time and resources needed to bring a secure product to the market (aided by a C&A program), has shown that to make financial sense even in industries like Insurance, Banking, Asset Management and Pharmaceuticals.

With the frequent network and data breaches in this high threat landscape, the C&A program can also bring accountability and awareness to the entire C-level and other executive leaders of a company by providing them visibility to the cyber maturity of their applications and systems within their IT environment and the cyber risk they may be carrying. The C&A process can give regulators information to pinpoint who is responsible for security weaknesses or failures, whether resulting from underinvestment in security, the lack of attention to expired ATO's or incomplete POA&Ms, or other issues.

While CISOs go above and beyond implementing various security concepts like Defense in Depth and Zero Trust to try to provide compensating and mitigating controls, they must not be held responsible for security breaches resulting from cybersecurity underinvestment or from the business' acceptance of undue levels of risk. The C&A program is an excellent way to make leaders throughout the company true stakeholders in responsible cyber risk management [2], especially with the regulator's window into how the risk postures of individual leaders affect security risks and outcomes.

5 Definitions

CIS – stands for center of internet standards. It is generally used to refer to the universally recognized best security practices for the hardening and securing of IT systems and data to provide protection from vulnerability exploits and cyber-attacks.

GRC – stands for governance, risk management, and compliance. It is generally used to refer to the strategy (and the tooling) used to manage an organization's governance, (operational and enterprise) risk management, and compliance with local, state, and federal regulations, and company security policies and standards.

NIST – stands for National Institute of Standards and Technology. It is a non-regulatory US entity within the US Department of Commerce with the mission to promote innovation and industrial competitiveness.

OEM – stands for Original Equipment Manufacturer. In the context of software, this is the entity that creates the original version of the large and complex software (e.g., Microsoft is the OEM for Windows OS, and Oracle for its relational database) and sells licenses for private and business use [3].

POA&M – stands for plan of action and milestones. It is a plan that details the steps to be taken to fix the issues found while performing a security control assessment during a certification and accreditation exercise. It identifies all the tasks required to fix the issue(s) identified, the resources (i.e., personnel and time) required to complete the tasks, and the timetable for completion.

Disclaimer

The views expressed and commentary provided in this chapter are strictly private and do not represent the opinions or work or the state of implementations or practices within the cyber-security or IT programs of my current or former employer(s).

References

1. NIST Joint Task Force (2018). NIST Special Publication 800-37 Revision 2 – Risk Management Framework for Information Systems and Organizations: A System Life Cycle Approach for Security and Privacy. https://nvlpubs.nist.gov/nistpubs/SpecialPublications/NIST.SP.800-37r2.pdf Accessed 11 Mar 2021
2. Moore S (2021) Gartner Predicts 40% of Boards Will Have a Dedicated Cybersecurity Committee by 2025 https://www.gartner.com/en/newsroom/press-releases/2021-01-28-gartner-predicts-40%2D%2Dof-boards-will-have-a-dedicated- Accessed March 10, 2021
3. Badhwar (2021) The CISO's Next Frontier: AI, Post-Quantum Cryptography and Advanced Security Paradigms (Springer)

Further Reading

Grance T, Hash J, et al (2002) Security Guide for Interconnecting Information Technology Systems. https://nvlpubs.nist.gov/nistpubs/Legacy/SP/nistspecialpublication800-47.pdf Accessed 11 Mar 2021

Agile Insider blog (2020) What Is a POAM? https://www.agileit.com/news/what-is-a-poam/ Accessed 11 Mar 2021

Douvres N (2021) Understand the risk management framework (RMF). https://www.aemcorp.com/managedservices/blog/understanding-the-risk-management-framework. Accessed 11 March 2021

CIS (2021) CIS Controls. https://www.cisecurity.org/controls/. Accessed 11 Mar 2021

Wikipedia (2021) DoD Information Assurance Certification and Accreditation Process (DIACAP). https://en.wikipedia.org/wiki/Department_of_Defense_Information_Assurance_Certification_and_Accreditation_Process. Accessed 11 Mar 2021

Radziwill N and Benton M (2018) Cybersecurity Cost of Quality: Managing the Costs of Cybersecurity Risk Management https://arxiv.org/ftp/arxiv/papers/1707/1707.02653.pdf. Accessed March 13 2021

Wallix Blog. Cost of a Data Breach vs. Cost of a Security Solution http://blog.wallix.com/cost-of-a-data-breach-response. Accessed 11 Mar 2021

Swinhoe D (2020) What is the cost of a data breach? https://www.csoonline.com/article/3434601/what-is-the-cost-of-a-data-breach.html . Accessed 11 Mar 2021

Moore S (2020) Gartner Predicts 75% of CEOs Will be Personally Liable for Cyber-Physical Security Incidents by 2024 https://www.gartner.com/en/newsroom/press-releases/2020-09-01-gartner-predicts-75%2D%2Dof-ceos-will-be-personally-liabl . Accessed March 5 2021.

Hack Back or Not?

1 Introduction

The toll on global economy from cybercrime attacks and breaches has been estimated to be a whopping 945 Billion dollars. If you add the cost of adding new or updating legacy cybersecurity infrastructure and services including cybersecurity personnel, the then price tag is almost a trillion dollars, according to a recent McAfee report [1].

The same report estimates the loss of business and productivity from the downtime caused by cyber security incidents and breaches cost the businesses between $100,000 and $500,000 per incident. The longer downtime incidents were more damaging. The average cost to organizations from their longest amount of downtime in 2019 was $762,231 per incident.

Given the losses, there is a case to be made that rather than being on the receiving end of these cyber-attacks and breaches, why not launch a counterattack, known in the industry as hack back, on the malicious entities perpetrating these attacks?

This chapter provides a discussion on this matter in greater detail.

2 Genesis

Some businesses may decide that enough is enough and may want to hack back to retrieve exfiltrated data. Some may want to garnish or take back the ransom they paid.

There is at least one congressman who supported a bill [3] that would protect an individual or company if they were to hack back a perpetrator of cybercrime.

© The Author(s), under exclusive license to Springer Nature
Switzerland AG 2021
R. Badhwar, *The CISO's Transformation*,
https://doi.org/10.1007/978-3-030-81412-0_23

The intent of the bill was "to provide a defense to prosecution for fraud and related activity in connection with computers for persons defending against unauthorized intrusions into their computers" [2].

Introduced on June 13, 2019, in a previous session of US Congress, the bill died when it did not receive a vote. However, the intent was clear. As the losses mount from cyberattacks, there may be similar bills in the future.

The United States (US) government or US based businesses are not the sole targets, the entire world is feeling the brunt of these attacks. There may be other global entities or even nation states that may consider a "hack back."

The next couple of sections make the case of why NOT to engage in hack back (or equivalent) activities.

3   What Is a Hack Back?

A hack back can a defined as any activity meant to

(a) Launch a counter cyber attack on an individual, group or even a nation state
(b) Retrieve or take possession of stolen artifacts including exfiltrated data, documents, and bitcoin or other forms of cryptocurrency
(c) Cause disruption to the computing infrastructure used by the attackers to carry out their hacking activities
(d) Identify the attacker(s) and report them to law enforcement agencies – local (e.g., FBI) or global (e.g., Interpol), as the case may be.

4   Security Issues and Impediments

If we are a nation of laws, and also belong to a coalition of nations that work together, then why hasn't anything been done about these hackers that remain at large, is a question that many victims are asking. Why aren't our law enforcement agencies catching these hackers?

Given that most of the western world is very tech savvy, with sophisticated tools and state-of-the-art technology, then we should be able to stop these threat actors and malicious entities, right?

And in many cases, even if a hacker is caught or a dark web marketplace brought down, what was lost is now irretrievable, most of the bitcoin paid as ransoms or stolen from wallets, or the data artifacts exfiltrated, are not returned, adding to the frustration of the entities impacted.

Trust me the cyber security teams worldwide are trying very hard to detect and block these attacks but have fallen short for reasons described below.

4.1   Currency

The term currency is used to define the lifecycle of a given product, where N is used to denote the current version. Anything older than N-2 is generally considered out of currency. Product vendors generally stop issuing security patches and feature/ functionality updates for out of currency items.

A lot of the systems and software that (many) companies and government organizations run are out of currency, maybe due to financial constraints or maybe their upgrades have not been prioritized, which means that the OEMs do not issues security patches for any vulnerabilities that may be found in these specific versions, making them vulnerable to cyber-attacks.

(Trust me, if you fix the currency problem and keep your systems upgraded and patched then that alone would dramatically reduce your risk of being breached by a cyber attacker.)

4.2   Code Vulnerabilities

Given the shortage of qualified software developers [5, 6] and the faster delivery times to stay relevant in the very competitive business environment [10], the quality of code that is delivered by developers has been found to be substandard [8, 9].

The reason for the poor quality of code is directly attributable to the lack of experienced developers and software architects, the compressed timelines of code delivery, poor coding practices like copying code from untrusted sources on the internet, sharing of software libraries from unverifiable sources that have not been vetted by security tams, lack of quality control and checks, and the lack of (security) training on how to write secure code.

The problem is further exacerbated by the lack of vulnerability scanning of the code source during development and unit testing, or even as a last resort during the QA cycles. The primary focus of the developers has been found to be feature and functionality testing to meet the business requirements and needs within the aggressive delivery schedules.

All this leads to the leakage of many application vulnerabilities into production, which are then exploited by threat actors. Boom, game over.

4.3   The Weak Link

Humans have proven to be weakest link in our collective efforts to protect our systems from cyber attackers. Due to lack of proper training on how to recognize the malicious entities, compounded by the lack of security awareness, individual employees are often easy targets. Cyber attackers phish and spoof emails to steal user credentials. Attackers then use these stolen credentials to gain entry to corporate systems. With a foothold into our corporate networks, they generally move laterally to take control over key systems.

This problem is further exacerbated by the lack of multi-factor authentication (MFA) for many of our key high-risk systems, sites, portals, and internet exposed digital properties.

4.4   Sophisticated Attackers

Gone are the days of a hacker trying to break into company networks from their mother's garage. Today's cyber attackers are very sophisticated and educated, and belong to very well-funded and highly organized groups motivated by financial gain, social or political causes, or hacktivist missions. Many of them are members of elite cyber units (generally referred to advanced persistent threat (APT)) belonging to nation states, interested in espionage or intellectual property theft.

Under-resourced security teams of individual business entities are not a match for the sophistication and resources of APT. It's as if they were bringing a stick to a gunfight. If weaknesses and vulnerabilities across an entire network and application stack are not addressed, and if company employees are not trained on basic security hygiene, then all security teams cannot prevent the possibility of attack. All they can do is react to cyberattack events. It's as if they were putting their fingers in the dike to stop a flood. Threat actors just have to find one vulnerability or weakness to overtake a company network.

4.5   Lack of Defense Coordination

The US federal government agencies such as the NSA, CISA, DHS, FBI, the Secret Service, and Cyber command by far have more resources, skilled personnel, and threat intelligence than any other entity in the world. They have good intel on threat actors and have done a pretty decent job of protecting the government agencies (but for a few incidents). However, a lot of this information is classified and thus cannot be easily shared with commercial and private sector cyber security teams. Even if the information can be shared, the process to declassify information is slow and onerous, and the intel is not very effective by the time it is provided to commercial and private company cybersecurity teams and their CISOs.

Unlike certain far east countries, the security apparatus in the western world is decentralized. There is no central firewall or network, and every entity is responsible for the safety of their own networks and ecosystems. Almost all the 17 USG defense agencies have their own security apparatus and staff and, for good reason, also do not have centralized firewalls and shared networks. Most commercial or private financial services entities run their own networks and are responsible for the security of their own systems. While this decentralization works well to enable the concept of zero trust and separation of controls, it does not allow for the pooling of resources and threat intelligence, allowing for the threat actors to find weaknesses in individual company networks and systems.

4.6 Hacking Tools

The easy availability of hacking and network scanning tools like MimiKatz, hash-cat, shodan, nmap along with other hacking paraphernalia, rootkits, and ransom-ware kits on the dark web, has made even the novice hacker very potent, much to the chagrin of cyber security professionals and teams around the globe. The combined use of these tools with network anonymizers can be lethal. Also, with stolen user and admin credentials, ssh keys and certificates available on the dark web, attackers gain residence into a company's corporate network or applications with an ease which belies their disastrous intentions.

5 Making the Case

I recommend that individual users and business entities stay away from trying to hack-back for the reasons discussed below.

5.1 Hacker Identities Are Unknown

Most of the hackers or APT use sophisticated network identity obfuscation capabilities to hid their true identity (i.e., IP address, location, etc.).

Most of the attackers use VPN riding on Tor (anonymizer) for network connectivity and generally launch attacks from virtual servers (or containers) hosted on short-lived virtual servers on obscure dark web domains. This makes the attackers anonymous and it is almost impossible to discover and hunt them. Hacking back these entities is simply not very feasible.

5.2 It May Be Illegal

The whole reason the congressman from Georgia was trying to pass a bill was to provide some grounds of legal protection to cybersecurity personnel who may want to hack back. To hack back is to engage in vigilantism.

In the *Best Practices for Victim Response and Reporting of Cyber Incidents* published by the US DOJ, the Cybersecurity Unit recommends that victims "Do Not Hack into or Damage Another Network."

They further state that:

> A victimized organization should not attempt to access, damage, or impair another system that may appear to be involved in the intrusion or attack. Regardless of motive, doing so is likely illegal, under U.S. and some foreign laws, and could result in civil and/or criminal liability [4].

In addition, one should also get familiar with 18 U.S. Code § 1030 – Fraud and related activity in connection with computers [5] which may prohibit illegal or unauthorized access to a computer. This would apply both to the hackers, and those who hack back.

In my opinion, trying to respond to a criminal activity with another potential criminal act not only puts the hack-backer into legal jeopardy, but may also create legal and financial liability for their employer.

For these reasons, the security training and awareness program must very clearly call out the (defensive) posture that cybersecurity incident responders must take while responding to a security incident.

They must engage their legal and compliance teams to share any information they may have gathered about the identities of the cyber-attackers and the location (e.g., IP addresses, domain names etc.) of the (dark web) infrastructure used for the malicious activities or attacks, with law enforcement agencies.

5.3 Open Cyber-Warfare

Even if you have the skillset to conduct a hack-back operation, such an act can have unintended consequences.

Hacking back a hacker or a hacking syndicate can instigate a counter-attack, leading to cyber warfare that could be even more destructive and damaging to the economies of the various businesses or (even) countries involved.

The fact of the matter is that the mobility and anonymity of cyber attackers give them an upper hand in open cyber warfare. Additionally, we really don't want corporate security teams attacking nation states, without understanding the ramifications, quite possibly adversely affecting US diplomacy.

5.4 Friendly Fire

Cyber-attacks are often launched from compromised machines or hosts belonging to other companies or business entities without the knowledge or against the will of the actual owners. A hack back attack may damage the infrastructure of another business entity, university, or country, causing legal liability for those who hack back and their employer.

5.5 Asset Retrieval

It is very hard to retrieve any financial assets stolen from business entities. Any data that was exfiltrated is generally encrypted using 256-bit cryptographic algorithms. Even if it is retrieved, it next to impossible to confirm its viability unless a decryption key is available.

6 The CISO Take

My recommendation is that individuals and business entities do not engage in a hack-back or equivalent operation. It is a high-risk low-reward game, and I would not want to play it. Sometimes a well-calculated and planned out defensive posture is better than blind offense. I recommend you contact and trust the law enforcement agencies and let them do their jobs to stop threat actors from their hacking activities.

I also recommend that you do what is totally in your control: implement Zero Trust with least privilege; deploy a defense-in-depth security stack; patch all your critical, high, and medium risk vulnerabilities in 0, 30, and 60 days, respectively; train your workforce to recognize phishing attacks; protect and manage your identities; and hire a CISO with the leadership skills, the technical expertise, and the acumen to steer your business ship safely through the murky waters of high cyber risk.

This is yet another reason why companies need CISOs on their board of directors. A board informed by expert advice and prudent counsel on how to respond to cyberattacks will be more likely to provide appropriate mitigation of cyber and reputational risk.

7 Definitions

APT – stands for Advanced Persistent Threat. It is used to describe a campaign of attacks by persistent sophisticated threat actors whose intent is to gain long-term residence or presence on the network of the target. The list of malicious activities includes but is not limited to stealing intellectual property or company sensitive data, sabotaging key network segments or systems, installing and operating backdoors to communicate with CnC servers, and conducting complete site takeovers. These attacks are complex, targeted, well-resourced and funded, and are generally conducted by nation states or other criminal organizations.

The Dark Web – is that part of the deep web that is only accessible by using a web anonymizer (Dark Net). The websites on the dark web run on hidden services and are identified with Onion addresses, where the clients and onion sites negotiate rendezvous points to establish a connection. The IP addresses of the servers that host the websites on the dark web are hidden (masked) and also transient (short-lived) in nature. The dark web is generally used for illegal activities or criminal enterprises but could also be used by reporters, whistle-blowers, and dissidents in authoritarian countries [11].

Defense in Depth – is an approach of deploying layered security controls to protect sensitive data and systems. The cybersecurity layered controls could be further broken down as perimeter security controls, networks security controls, application security controls, data security controls, and endpoint security controls. In some instances, they are also defined as the layered controls for (3 tier) application architecture (presentation, application, and data tiers).

Zero Trust – is a security architecture and implementation paradigm that reduces enterprise risk by performing secure implementations in compliance with the principal that all assets inside and outside a perimeter firewall are not to be trusted and thus access control for users, devices, systems and services must be provided using least privilege.

References

1. Smith Z M and Lostri E (2020) The Hidden Costs of Cybercrime. https://www.mcafee.com/enterprise/en-us/assets/reports/rp-hidden-costs-of-cybercrime.pdf. Accessed 1 Mar 2021
2. H.R. 3270 (116th): Active Cyber Defense Certainty Act. https://www.govtrack.us/congress/bills/116/hr3270. Accessed 1 Mar 2021
3. H.R. 3270 (116th): Active Cyber Defense Certainty Act Text. https://www.govtrack.us/congress/bills/116/hr3270/text Accessed 1 Mar 2021
4. Department of Justice. Best Practices for Victim Response and Reporting of Cyber Incidents. https://www.justice.gov/sites/default/files/opa/speeches/attachments/2015/04/29/criminal_division_guidance_on_best_practices_for_victim_response_and_reporting_cyber_incidents.pdf. Accessed 1 Mar 2021
5. Cornell Law School. 18 U.S. Code § 1030 – Fraud and related activity in connection with computers. https://www.law.cornell.edu/uscode/text/18/1030#e_2. Accessed 1 Mar 2021
6. Morgan S (2019). Cybersecurity Talent Crunch to Create 3.5 Million Unfilled Jobs Globally By 2021 https://cybersecurityventures.com/jobs/ Accessed 1 Mar 2021
7. Rogers K, Spring B (2020). We are outnumbered' — cybersecurity pros face a huge staffing shortage as attacks surge during the pandemic https://www.cnbc.com/2020/09/05/cyber-security-workers-in-demand.html Accessed 1 Mar 2021
8. 5 Things Responsible for Your Poor Code Quality https://blog.submain.com/5-things-responsible-poor-code-quality/ Accessed 2 Mar 2021
9. Giese D (2015) Software's Hidden Demon: Poor Code Quality https://innolitics.com/articles/code-quality/ Accessed 2 Mar 2021
10. Laukkanena E, Itkonena J, Lasseniusba C (2017) Problems, causes and solutions when adopting continuous delivery – A systematic literature review https://www.sciencedirect.com/science/article/pii/S0950584916302324 Accessed 2 Mar 2021
11. Badhwar (2021) The CISO's Next Frontier: AI, Post-Quantum Cryptography and Advanced Security Paradigms (Springer)

Further Reading

Giles M (2019) Five reasons "hacking back" is a recipe for cybersecurity chaos. https://www.technologyreview.com/2019/06/21/134840/cybersecurity-hackers-hacking-back-us-congress/.

Freedberg S (2019) Don't Hack Back: Call The FBI & They'll Call NSA. https://breakingdefense.com/2019/09/dont-hack-back-call-the-fbi-theyll-call-nsa/.

Imperva, Learning Center Resources. Advanced persistent threat (APT), https://www.imperva.com/learn/application-security/apt-advanced-persistent-threat/. Accessed 13 Dec 2020

Novatech DynaSis. The Price of Security: How Much Does a Cybersecurity Attack Actually Cost? https://dynasis.com/2019/03/price-security-how-much-cybersecurity-attack-actually-cost.

CISOs Need Liability Protection

1 Making the Case

Some of you may know that a criminal complaint has been brought by the US attorney of Northern California against Joe Sullivan, the former Chief Security Officer (CSO) of the ride-sharing firm Uber, for failure to disclose a data breach to the U.S. Federal Trade Commission (FTC) while it was investigating a 2014 data breach at Uber. Joe was the CSO of Uber from April 2015 to November 2017 and is currently the CISO of internet technology provider Cloudflare.

I'm not a lawyer and the intent of this chapter is not to argue for or against this legal matter between the FTC and Joe, (not to) provide any legal advice, or (not) pass any judgment against a case pending in front a court of law. Rather, the intent is to highlight the potential precedent set by this case or any judgment to hold all CISOs and CSOs financially and criminally liable for data or network breaches occurring on their watch for a current or any previous position, and to recommend best practices for improving liability protection and indemnification.

The four commonly used indemnification techniques available to CISO/CSOs (and other senior executives) are discussed below.

2 Liability Insurance

In the corporate world, there is an insurance vehicle called directors and officer's (D&O) liability insurance that is generally used to protect directors or officers of a given business from personal financial losses and criminal liability if they are sued in their professional capacity. This insurance vehicle generally covers legal costs and fees, and any other costs incurred from such a suit.

© The Author(s), under exclusive license to Springer Nature
Switzerland AG 2021
R. Badhwar, *The CISO's Transformation*,
https://doi.org/10.1007/978-3-030-81412-0_24

One key point to note here is that generally this coverage is only available through employers and is not something that a CISO can purchase on their own either solely or as additional incremental coverage.

The D&O coverage is the primary mechanism to protect directors and officers, but given the exponentially higher risk from financial or criminal liability stemming from data breaches or punitive and enforcement actions by regulators, there are certain finer points one must clarify with the insurer before deeming this sufficient protection for oneself.

2.1   Verify Your Coverage

1. While I am not an expert in D&O underwriting, there could be instances where the insurance policy may use terms such as 'insured persons' to allude to company directors and officers. The CISO/CSO must explicitly verify if they are considered a company officer or director. If there is any ambiguity in the response, then CISOs/CSOs must insist that the policies specifically mention them as named individuals rather than cover them under generic terms.
2. The CISO/CSO must inquire about loss coverage for cybersecurity events and/ or incidents. For example, loss coverage should include regulator or customer suits stemming from data breaches or privacy violations from exposure of sensitive data, individual fines by regulators, civil or class action lawsuits, and stockholder suits. The CISO/CSO must also be covered for lawsuits by other (past and present) company officers or the company itself.
3. The CISO/CSO must verify which types of events would trigger a claim for coverage and ascertain the maximum period within which a notice must be provided to the insurance company for the coverage to begin.
4. The CISO/CSO must verify that cybersecurity events fall within the scope of the policy. Just adding the CISO as a named entity to the D&O coverage may not be useful if cyber events are excluded from the policy.
5. Lastly, the CISO/CSO must understand what items are excluded from coverage (e.g., regulatory or criminal matters). They must also be aware of any exclusions that may get added during (annual) policy renewal.

3   Employment Contracts

An employment contract is the document that stipulates the contract within the company and the new employee. Generally, these contracts are written by the hiring company and most prospective new hires never get it reviewed by an employment attorney.

1. Ideally speaking, before assuming a CISO role, a candidate should hire an employment lawyer to verify that provisions for appropriate liability protections are written into the employment contract.
2. This is also the point in time when the CISO should confirm that they are indeed considered an officer of the company by ensuring that it is clearly stipulated in the contract and that the company would stand behind them in case of any litigation arising from cybersecurity-driven incidents. (This may not hold true for junior CISOs or BISOs, but regardless they must inquire about the needed protections that can be provided to them).
3. If a CISO does not pursue contract review prior to employment, they can still proactively seek contract clarifications and request changes. (Most employers are generally willing to do what is right to ensure that the intrinsic hazards of assuming CISO responsibilities do not translate into CISOs having to fear undue assumption of personal liability). (The companies should also realize that their ability to hire top talent may be hampered if they do not provide proper protections and indemnification coverage to the CISO).

4   State Laws

Because indemnification laws vary by state, CISOs must be aware of the indemnification requirements or stipulations for the states in which their firms are incorporated. Some states may grant more power to firms to change how they indemnify their officers than other states.

I recommend that CISOs gain awareness about these state laws [1, 2], and associated issues [3], as there are some states with stricter indemnification laws than others, this would help the CISO (and directors and officers) avoid assumption of undue personal liability and risk.

5   Company Bylaws

The Company bylaws are a resource for understanding a company's indemnification policy. CISOs must be familiar with their company bylaws as they apply to the indemnification of their liability. They must also be aware that the bylaws can be changed, and that those changes are only discussed at the executive leadership committee (ELC) level (generally only the CEO and the CEO's direct reports). CISOs who do sit on the company ELC must try to influence any Bylaw edits or modifications to also incorporate stipulations that may provide them the needed protections and also prevent any modifications that may weaken the said coverage. CISOs who do not sit on the ELC may not be informed about any changes that may have an adverse effect on their protection, in which case it is thus recommended that the CISO conduct regular (quarterly or at least annual) reviews of these bylaws and discuss any concerns with the legal department if needed.

6 The CISO Take

Most CISOs I know, go above and beyond to protect the companies they serve, from malicious entities (both internal and external), cyber attackers, malware, hacktivists and advanced persistent threat, by ensuring that the needed security controls have been implemented to maintain the integrity, confidentiality and availability of company sensitive data and systems.

Having said that, due to distributed nature of the modern IT systems leading to inherent complexity, rapid migration to the cloud, the number of critical and high-risk vulnerabilities discovered almost on a daily basis in common operating systems and application software and hardware, and the emergence of sophisticated cyber attackers with a vested interest to gain financially by breaching corporate assets and systems, not all systems can be protected from compromises. Also, the lack of available funding to the cybersecurity teams to improve their defensive postures, adds to the difficulty of timely patching all known vulnerabilities.

If a data or network breach were to occur, then it is my advice that the CISOs must make the appropriate disclosures to the regulators and other local, state or federal government entities, and end users or customers in consultation and partnership with their legal and compliance departments. They must understand the applicable breach disclosure laws and abide by them fully.

Given the enactment and subsequent enforcement of many recent local, state or federal data protection and privacy laws, the CISOs may sometimes find themselves unprotected from liability stemming from system and network breaches, sensitive data exfiltration, unauthorized access of sensitive systems or data, and third-party attacks for the previously mentioned reasons.

It is thus my recommendation that CISOs take this issue very seriously and ensure that they have the appropriate coverage and indemnity from any liability they may be subject to while they are doing their jobs to provide the best protection possible within the technical and financial constraints, they may operate in.

7 Definitions

Cyber Event – refers to any event or malicious activity that may result in an unauthorized access, disclosure, destruction, or exfiltration of company sensitive data, the spread of malware on a company network, or cause financial or reputation harm.

Disclaimer
The views expressed and commentary provided in this chapter are strictly private and do not represent the opinions of my current or former employer(s). Any advice provided here must not be construed as legal advice. If you choose to follow any advice provided in this book, then you must do so at your own risk.

References

1. The American Subcontractors Association, Inc. (2019). https://www.keglerbrown.com/content/uploads/2019/10/Anti-Indemnity-Statutes-in-the-50-States-2020.pdf, Accessed 15 April 2021
2. Allison L, Carl T et al (2021) Indemnification Considerations for Directors and Officers of Delaware Entities https://www.skadden.com/insights/publications/2021/02/indemnification-considerations Accessed April 18, 2021
3. John F. Olson, Jonathan C. Dickey et al (2013) Director and Officer Indemnification and Insurance–Issues for Public Companies to Consider https://www.gibsondunn.com/director-and-officer-indemnification-and-insurance-issues-for-public-companies-to-consider/ Accessed 20 April 2021

Further Reading

Brumfield C (2020) New state privacy and security laws explained: Is your business ready? https://www.csoonline.com/article/3429608/11-new-state-privacy-and-security-laws-explained-is-your-business-ready.html Accessed on April 15, 2021

Tollefson R (2019) Which states have the toughest privacy laws? https://resources.infosecinstitute.com/topic/which-states-have-toughest-privacy-laws/, Accessed on April 15, 2021

Yannella P et al (2019) Delaware and New Hampshire Join Growing List of States with New Insurance Data Security Laws https://www.natlawreview.com/article/delaware-and-new-hampshire-join-growing-list-states-new-insurance-data-security-laws Accessed on April 15, 2021

Schwartz MJ (2020) Implications for CSOs of Charges Against Joe Sullivan. https://www.bankinfosecurity.com/implications-for-csos-charges-against-joe-sullivan-a-14900Accessed 10 Apr 2021

KAGAN J (2019) Directors and Officers Liability Insurance https://www.investopedia.com/terms/d/directors-and-officers-liability-insurance.asp Accessed 10 Apr 2021

Radcliff D (2020) Uber breach case a 'watershed moment' for CISOs' liability risk https://www.csoonline.com/article/3584071/uber-breach-case-a-watershed-moment-for-cisos-liability-risk.html Accessed 10 Apr 2021

Pollard J et al (2020) It's Never the Data Breach – It's Always the Cover-Up https://go.forrester.com/blogs/its-never-the-data-breach-its-always-the-cover-up/ Accessed 10 Apr 2021

Clouse K (2018) Why Executives Should Negotiate an Indemnity Clause into Employment Agreements https://clousebrown.com/indemnity-clauses/ Accessed on April 15, 2021

LaCroix K (2018) Limits on Indemnification and Advancement for Delaware Corporations https://www.dandodiary.com/2018/06/articles/indemnification-and-advancement/limits-indemnification-advancement-delaware-corporations/ Accessed on April 18, 2021

Enable Secure Work-From-Home

1 Making the Case

In this book's last chapter, I have shared a picture (Fig. 1) that was drawn by my 15 year old daughter. Sometimes pictures say things better than words.

The years 2020 and 2021 have been plagued by the global pandemic. The impact from the novel coronavirus (Covid-19) has been devastating to the world's economy. This global Pandemic has forced the business continuity management (BCM) protocol for each company to go into effect, testing each company's capability for normal, disruption-free business operations.

Apart from the need for redundant, highly available and disaster recoverable IT infrastructure, human capital is key to a successful BCM strategy for any global or local company. If the employees and users cannot go into the traditional office and work facilities due to travel restrictions stemming from a local viral outbreak or global pandemic, then in an effort to maintain normal business operations, they must all be able to continue to SECURELY work from home or other remote locations without compromising the confidentiality and integrity of business sensitive data and operations [1].

So, while I give all the kudos to the medical professionals and other first responders in our cities and communities that are fighting the spread of the novel corona virus, I would also like to tip my hat and acknowledge the good work done by the cyber security professionals for helping to enable the secure work-from-home paradigm for corporate America and around the globe!

Due to hard work and ingenuity of the cyber security and IT professionals, almost the entire world was and still is working remotely from their respective homes without any tangible or noticeable impact to most business operations or level of service.

© The Author(s), under exclusive license to Springer Nature
Switzerland AG 2021
R. Badhwar, *The CISO's Transformation*,
https://doi.org/10.1007/978-3-030-81412-0_25

Fig. 1 Cyber teamwork

(Additional details on the how-to and the various technologies used to securely work from home are detailed in my other book – The CISO's Next Frontier, published by Springer) [1].

2   The CISO Take

It is an undeniable truth that the cybersecurity professionals have enabled the capability for the IT and Business teams to securely work from home by either adding new capabilities or improving up and hardening the various remote connectivity and collaboration technologies.

We have further strengthened the faith within the minds of the business leaders of the world that secure work from home is indeed possible, and the world will never be the same again. This is evident from the various announcements around the globe where companies are all changing their postures and are going to allow a much larger percentage of employees to work from home than what they did before, even after we have conquered this virus (by the end of 2021).

This will not only enable the businesses to add flexibility to the work schedules of their employees, decrease worldwide pollution from car emissions, improve health of employees, promote better family interactions by being able to spend more times with near and dear ones, it will also the improve the diversity and inclusion posture of our workforce by opening new doors and employment opportunities to many members of our community (e.g., many mom's that could not work because they were taking care of their kids at home, or had to be at home to returning kids from school every afternoon).

In this new world we will continue to enable the business and have a more diverse and flexible work force – all this without compromising our mission to maintain the confidentiality, integrity and availability of our data and systems.

References

1. Badhwar (2021) The CISO's Next Frontier: AI, Post-Quantum Cryptography and Advanced Security Paradigms (Springer)

Further Reading

Although this chapter is about the pandemic induced secure work from home paradigm, I recommend that you also check out the article below on Chief Shannon Kent. She was a member of the IC and CT community, was one of the first women in the US Special Operations Force (SOF), spoke multiple languages, and took part in many human intel gathering (Mohawk) missions, and was assigned to a Navy Seal unit in Norfolk VA. Chief Kent was KIA on Jan 16, 2019 in Syria, while serving our nation. I know we cybersecurity folk are doing our best to protect our respective firms from various threat actors (internal and external) to the best of our abilities, but we need to not forget the sacrifices by our intel community colleagues. Until Valhalla, Chief Kent!

Skovlund M Jr (2019) THE LEGEND OF CHIEF SHANNON KENT https://coffeeordie.com/shannon-kent/ Accessed March 10, 2021

Postlude – Paying It Forward

This book has primarily focused on various cybersecurity leadership topics and my journey as a cybersecurity leader and technical writer. But as a postlude, I also want to very briefly talk about my private and personal quest to help find jobs for others in need. I believe this has helped me with my leadership journey and has also kept me grounded.

Over the years, I have focused my efforts to help find jobs for the veterans (who gave their all serving their country), women, other minorities, and other socially disadvantaged persons, that have struggled to find good employment. I have also helped some H-1B visa holders who only have 1–2 months to find a new job if they lose their jobs due to workforce reductions, or F-1 visa holders who look for jobs but do not have the good connections to give them that first opportunity. I have also pushed for F-1 students to be offered internship positions after I noticed that many companies would not offer it to them because they think they would need to file an H-1B visa for them if they were to try to hire them in the future. Although I have always complied with company policies when it comes to hiring professionally, at a personal level I have tried to help anyone that needs a job and asks for my assistance.

Cybersecurity and IT are areas with tremendous potential to provide employment to many. Given the large shortage of qualified workers, there is a tremendous opportunity to bring new and diverse talent into the cybersecurity fold. While I try to do this professionally to ensure that I can hire the most talented and diverse cybersecurity talent, I also try to open pathways at a private and personal level for persons that I cannot hire but who would benefit from my recommendation or coaching. I have done so by separating my professional and personal life, and only use my personal connections to do whatever I can ethically. We should avoid using our professional position to influence others, due to the potential for conflict of interest.

We are all very busy with our professional and personal lives and the pandemic has made matters worse, but we can all take a moment to perform little acts kindness to help other cybersecurity professionals or anyone else in need of gainful

© The Author(s), under exclusive license to Springer Nature
Switzerland AG 2021
R. Badhwar, *The CISO's Transformation*,
https://doi.org/10.1007/978-3-030-81412-0

employment. These actions don't require you to spend money or make donations: sometimes all it takes to help someone is to pick up the phone and call an acquaintance, send an email, or forward a Twitter or LinkedIn message to a someone you know who is hiring for an open job.

In my limited capacity, I have made a commitment to reach out to my cybersecurity network (on LinkedIn, Twitter or FB) and tell people that if they've been laid off or furloughed from their job, then they should let me know how I can help them. I can write them a recommendation, reach out to other security technologists that may be hiring, provide a referral, share career advice, provide coaching on security topics, or review their resume. I don't need anything in return. All I ask is that they do the same for other security technologists and others when they are able.

Here are some ways you can also help:

(a) Volunteer your time to teach or coach a returning veteran or unemployed cybersecurity community member to help them get a cybersecurity certification. Certifications not only help to increase the skillset of the candidate but also are the keys that open doors for jobs where security certifications set a minimum job application criterion.

(b) Keep an eye out for job postings on LinkedIn or Twitter. When you see something that has been posted by your connection or acquaintance, forward that link to the people you know who are looking for a job, but don't stop there. Follow up with a phone call (or email) to the hiring manager to ensure that you have helped established that connection between the two parties.

(c) I would like to reiterate that most jobs in the industry are filled through recommendations and word-of-mouth marketing. Every little bit we can do goes a long way to achieve the goal of connecting the job seekers with the hiring managers.

(d) Pay it forward. These random little acts of kindness have a way of finding their way back and helping you out when may be down in need for a helping hand. Trust me, I know this from personal experience. There have been many instances in my life when friends, colleagues, and managers helped me find my next job or make that elusive connection with a key recruiter when I hadn't heard back from anyone after submitting many resumes (during the dotcom bust of 2000–2002). Being on an H-1B visa (almost two decades ago) did not make things any easier, but while there were many who made tactical decisions not to hire someone who needed sponsorship, there were some who made the strategic decision to hire me based on a good recommendation. It is now my time to recommend others who are being ignored by those tactical hiring managers trying to save some dollars or the hassle of sponsorship. There are also instances when I have observed folks pass over returning veterans, pregnant women, or people lacking *relevant* experiences or cybersecurity certifications. One lesson I have learned during my 26 years of doing this is that sometimes your gut tells you when you must hire if the applicant demonstrates hunger for learning and a passion for acquiring and applying cybersecurity skills, because the skill can be taught and the certification can be obtained later.

I hope I have made the case for you to consider helping job seekers. Do it without expecting anything in return, and I guarantee that the satisfaction of seeing that joy on someone's face or gleam in their eyes knowing that they can provide for themselves and/or their family, is really worth it.

Best,

-Raj

Index

0-9, and Symbols
1:1, 110

A
Access control list (ACL), 50
Access point (AP), 126, 127
Active Directory (AD), 61, 63, 81
Advanced persistent threat (APT), 4, 6, 8, 17,
        21, 26, 45, 68, 71, 106, 154, 155,
        157, 164
Anti-Virus (AV), 49, 52, 140
Applied behavioral analysis (ABA), 75
Artificial intelligence (AI), 5, 31, 39, 40, 45,
        75, 81, 83, 117
Asperger's, 75
Authorization to operate (ATO), 144, 146, 147
Authorization to operate with conditions
        (ATOC), 146
Autism spectrum disorder (ASD), 75

B
Bias-free, 79, 82, 83, 118
Biometric authentication, 17, 117, 126
Biometric recognition, 126
Blockchain, 39, 40, 42, 43
Blue screen of death (BSOD), 137, 139–141
Board-level participation, 17–18
Board of directors (BoD), 6, 7, 11, 12, 17, 25,
        32, 35, 57, 119, 157
Boot drive, 138–141
Bot (robot), 43, 92
Bricked, 137–141

Business continuity management (BCM), 6,
        29, 34, 35, 167
Business domain awareness, 97
Business information security officer
        (BISO), 33
Business resilience office (BRO), 34

C
California Consumer Privacy Act
        (CCPA), 12, 13
Career growth, 36, 89, 100, 111
Center of internet standards (CIS), 145, 147
Certificate authority (CA), 93, 94
Certification and accreditation (C&A), 51,
        118–119, 143–145, 147, 148
Certified ethical hacker (CEH), 31, 36
Certified Information Security Manager
        (CISM), 33
Certified Information Systems Security
        Professional (CISSP), 31, 32, 36,
        84, 111, 131, 134
Change Advisory Board (CAB), 92–94
Change management, 49–51, 92–94
Chief Legal Officer (CLO), 144
Chief risk officer (CRO), 18, 100, 101,
        119, 144
Chief security officer (CSO), 33, 34, 48, 126,
        161, 162
CISCO Certified Design Associate
        (CCDA), 31
CISCO Certified Internetwork Expert
        (CCIE), 31
CISCO Certified Network Professional
        (CCNP), 31

© The Author(s), under exclusive license to Springer Nature
Switzerland AG 2021
R. Badhwar, *The CISO's Transformation*,
https://doi.org/10.1007/978-3-030-81412-0

CISO maturity model (CMM), 29–36
Command and control (CnC) server, 9, 26, 59,
        60, 62, 71, 127
Common branch for business (CBB), 138, 141
Common Internet File System (CIFS), 49
Common Vulnerabilities and Exposures
        (CVE), 115, 116
Company bylaws, 163
Configuration Management Database
        (CMDB), 41
Continuous integration/continuous delivery
        (CI/CD), 92, 94, 117
Continuous monitoring, 146
Coronavirus disease (2019) (COVID-19), 131,
        132, 167
Corporate boards, 11–13
Counteroffers, 103–107
Cyber exceptionalism, 67, 68, 71, 100, 106
Cyber insurance, 6, 7, 12, 24–25
Cyber journey, 69–70
Cybersecurity and Infrastructure Security
        Agency (CISA), 33, 116, 119, 154
Cyber Security as a Service (CSaaS), 24
Cybersecurity Product Development, 23–24
Cybersecurity Services Development, 24
Cyber-warfare, 3, 68, 156
Cyber Wellness, 24

D
Data Loss Prevention (DLP), 49, 50,
        52, 84, 117
Date of Birth (DOB), 24
Defense security service (DSS), 12, 13
Deoxyribonucleic acid (DNA), 133
Department of Defense (DOD), 144
Department of Homeland Security (DHS), 46,
        116, 119, 154
Develop the talent, 95–99
Digital me, 39, 42
Directors and officers (D&O), 161–163
Disabilities, 73–75
Distributed Denial of Service (DDoS), 6, 9
DNS over HTTPS (DOH), 61
D&O coverage, 162
Domain controller (DC), 61
Domain Message Authentication Reporting
        and Conformance (DMARC),
        116, 119
Domain Name Service (DNS), 60–63, 91–94,
        117, 119, 127
Domain Name Service Secure (DNSSec), 117

Domain Name Service Sinkhole (DNS
        Sinkhole), 60, 62
Dynamic application security testing
        (DAST), 93, 94

E
Emergency Change Advisory Board
        (ECAB), 92
Employment contracts, 162–163
Employment lawyer, 163
Empowerment and enablement, 49–50
Enable asset protection, 118
Endpoint Detection and Response
        (EDR), 49, 52
Engineering management framework
        (EMF), 56
Executive CISO, 30, 35
Executive leadership committee (ELC), 163

F
Federal Financial Institutions Examination
        Council (FFIEC), 16
Federal Trade Commission (FTC), 161
Financial Industry Regulatory Authority
        (FINRA), 12, 16, 31
Financial Services Information Sharing and
        Analysis Center (FS-ISAC), 68, 116
Firewall (FW), 17, 40, 52, 83, 92, 93, 154, 158
Fraud Detection as a Service (FDaaS), 24
Friendly fire, 156–157

G
General Data Protection Regulation
        (GDPR), 12, 13
Golden Security Assertion Markup Language
        (Golden SAML), 61
Governance Risk and Compliance (GRC), 49,
        52, 118, 144, 146, 147
Guidance, 4, 5, 12, 13, 24, 46, 88, 109–112,
        137, 145

H
H1-B, 69, 70
Hack back, 151–158
Hacking tools, 155
Hands-on CISOs, 21, 34
Happiness, 87–89
Human element, 15–19
Hyper converged compute and storage, 39

Hyper Converged Infrastructure (HCI), 41

I

Identity and access management (IAM), 4,
    22, 45, 50
Indicators of compromise (IOC), 62, 68, 71,
    116, 132
Individual development plan (IDP), 111
Information Systems Security Architecture
    Professional (ISSAP), 32
Information Technology Infrastructure Library
    (ITIL), 31
Infrastructure as a Service (IaaS), 5, 22, 26, 93
Integrated Voice Response (IVR), 115
Intellectual property (IP), 3, 6, 8, 26, 45, 61,
    62, 71, 154–157
International Organization for Standardization
    (ISO), 16, 32, 36, 139
Internet of Things (IOT), 39–43
Intrusion Detection System (IDS), 116
Intrusion prevention system (IPS), 50, 52,
    116, 119

J

Job satisfaction, 87–89

K

Kill switches, 60, 63
Knowledge-based article (KBA), 117

L

Liability insurance, 161–162
Long-term servicing branch (LTSB), 138, 141
Long-term servicing channel (LTSC), 138, 141

M

Machine learning (ML), 31, 39, 40, 45, 60, 75,
    81, 120, 133
Man-in-the-Middle (MITM) attack, 41, 43
Master of Business Administration (MBA),
    33, 100, 101
Memory-driven computing, 39, 41
Mentors, 70, 88–89, 111
Mergers and acquisitions (M&A), 29, 35
Mission focus, 97
Mobile application management (MAM),
    125, 128
Mobile device management (MDM), 125, 128

Monitoring as a Service (MaaS), 24
Multi-factor authentication (MFA), 117, 119,
    126, 128, 154

N

National Football League (NFL), 15
National Institute of Standards and
    Technology (NIST), 16, 19, 32, 35,
    36, 52, 134, 144, 145, 147
Network access control (NAC), 41, 126
Network-attached Storage (NAS), 22, 118, 120
Network closet protection, 126
Network File System (NFS), 49
Network Time Protocol (NTP), 117
Network time protocol secure (NTPSec),
    117, 120
New York Department of Financial Services
    (NYDFS), 12, 13, 16, 19

O

Offensive Security Certified Professional
    (OSCP), 31, 36
Ohio State University (OSU), 15
One-time Password (OTP), 49
Operational ownership, 93, 94
Original equipment manufacturer (OEM), 148
Out of band (OOB), 117

P

Pass the hash (PTH), 61, 63
Personally identifiable information
    (PII), 24, 26
Plan of action and milestones (POA&M),
    144, 146–148
Platform as a Service (PaaS), 5, 93
Post-Traumatic Stress Disorder (PTSD), 70
Power of Inclusion, 82
Privileged access management (PAM), 49, 52
Problem solving, 98

Q

Quality Assurance (QA), 91, 92, 153
Quantify cyber risk, 5–6
Quantum computing, 39, 41, 133

R

Rapid influenza diagnostic test (RIDT), 133
Reconsider DOH, 61

Recovery drive, 138–141
Recovery media, 138, 139
Reduce threat surface, 116–117
Remote wipe, 125
Removal of conflict of interest, 48
Request for Comments (RFC), 33
Request for Information (RFI), 33
Request for Proposal (RFP), 22
Resource Access Control Facility (RACF), 81
Ribonucleic acid (RNA), 133
Risk management framework (RMF), 144
Robotic process automation (RPA), 39, 42
Root cause analysis (RCA), 92
RSA Conference (RSAC), 100

S
SAFE, 40, 110, 118, 141
Science, Technology, Engineering and Math
    (STEM), 75
Secure hash algorithm (SHA), 134
Secure M&A
Secure work from home, 167–169
Securities and Exchange Commission (SEC),
    12, 13, 16
Security Assertion Markup Language
    (SAML), 61, 63
Security evangelism, 4–8
Security frameworks, 16
Security hygiene, 16, 25, 61, 126, 154
Security incident and event management
    (SIEM), 23, 60, 62, 63, 117, 127
Security leadership, 31, 51, 87
Security operations center (SOC), 69,
    71, 126–128
See something, do something, 45–52
See something, say something, 46–48, 51
Separation of roles and responsibilities, 50–51
Service provider (SP), 61, 63, 144
Severe acute respiratory syndrome–
        coronavirus 2 (SARS-
        COV-2), 131–133
Single Sign-On (SSO), 61, 63, 112, 117
Skip-level meetings, 112
Social security number (SSN), 24, 26
Software as a Service (SaaS), 5, 9
SolarWinds, 59–63
Special needs, 73–75
Storage area network (SAN), 22, 118, 120
Style guides, 82, 84
Switched Port Analyzer (SPAN), 60
System and Organization Controls (Report) 1
    (SOC 1), 21

System and Organization Controls (Report) 2
    (SOC 2), 21
System Center Configuration Manager
    (SCCM), 118, 120
Systems thinking, 97–98

T
Technical writing, 56
Technology aptitude, 96
Test Access Point (TAP), 60
Third-party risk, 4, 13, 61, 62
Third-party risk management
Threat intelligence, 17, 23, 62, 68, 127,
        154, 155
Threat Intelligence as a Service (TIaaS), 24
Tor, 155
Training and awareness, 15, 45–47, 51, 82,
        116, 156
Training and communication, 82
Transmission Control Protocol (TCP), 9, 127
Transparent Data Encryption (TDE), 49
Transport Layer Security (TLS), 50, 61

U
Unified Extensible Firmware Interface (UEFI),
        118, 120, 140, 141
Universal serial bus (USB), 47, 138–141
US Capitol, 125–128
User Datagram Protocol (UDP), 9, 127
User training, 6
User training and awareness, 118

V
Virtual private cloud (VPC), 22
Virtual Private Network (VPN), 155
Vulnerability patching, 48

W
Web Access Firewall (WAF), 26, 50, 52
Whole-disk encryption, 118, 128
Win the marketplace, 18, 31
Women and minorities, 7
World Health Organization (WHO), 133

Z
Zero trust, 4, 17, 31, 32, 35, 39–41, 46, 51, 52,
        117, 147, 155, 157, 158

Printed in the United States
by Baker & Taylor Publisher Services